Untamed Leadership

UNTAMED LEADERSHIP
A Journey Through the Instincts That Shape Us

Brent A. Carter, Ph.D.

 ENSO BOOKS
United States of America

The following works and images have been reprinted with permission.

Please Hear What I Am Saying. ©1966. Charles Finn.

Images are reprinted under extended licenses through:
Front cover: ©Fotosearch (Black Timber Wolf)
Back cover and internal: ©RF123, Ltd (Animal silhouettes)

All other credits appear in the *Notes* section.
Proofread by Pam Nordberg.

Cataloguing-in-Publication Data

Carter, Brent A., 1968 –
Untamed leadership: a journey through the instincts that shape us all
/ 1st ed.
p., cm.
ISBN-13: 978-09820185-4-5
1. Leadership   2. Organization   3. Executive ability   4. Creative ability
in business   I. Untamed Leadership.   II. Title

HD57.7.F444 2011   LCCN: 2009936468
658.4'092-dc22

Printed in the United States of America

TABLE OF CONTENTS

A portion of the proceeds from this book will help fund research
and conservation initiatives of the *Colorado Wolf & Wildlife Center,*
Wolf Conservation Center and *Cheyenne Mountain Zoo.*

DEDICATION

To my wife, daughter, and parents.

This project would not have been possible without
your extraordinary efforts over the past two years.

Thank you for your love and constant support.

PROLOGUE

Ad Fontes Gubernatio
(To the Sources of Leadership)

In the late fourteenth century, one fundamental te-net altered the course of medieval Europe. In Latin, it was called *ad fontes*, which literally means "to the fountains." Europeans sought a departure from the feudalistic ideologies that had seized them during the Dark Ages, and they embarked on a quest for deeper insights into philosophy, religion, mathematics, cul-ture, fine arts, science, and the complexities of human behavior.

At that time in history, *ad fontes* embodied a navi-gational bearing pointing to the wisdom and insight of the ancient Greeks and Romans—and as this move-ment spread north from Italy, Europeans attempted to reflect not only the architecture and cultural amenities of ancient life but also the impressions and interpreta-tions of a new form of classical thinking. From philos-ophy to civics, from music to art, from science to the study of behavior, the Renaissance had begun. Pervad-ing nearly every echelon and compartment of society, this three-hundred year rebirth escalated a paradigm

1

shift in the lives of individuals. Rather than becoming literate through the church, people began educating each other. Rather than being secluded to a myopic perspective of the world, common folk became more involved in politics and merchandising beyond their village communities.[1] Their innate desires for reflection and metamorphosis instigated new societal and cultural norms. Europe had collectively changed direction by drinking from a new fountain. Consequently, the profound impacts of the Renaissance have spread to our own western civilization today in the foundational and ideological geometry that makes up our buildings, laws, commerce, rights as citizens, and approaches to understanding the world around us.

When we look at twenty-first-century organizations, we see the need for a similar renaissance. We need change. We need rebirth. Whether we govern a country, provide humanitarian or spiritual aid, deliver products or services to market, or support military missions that protect the lives and rights of others, we need a leadership reality that is a significant, cohesive, and comprehensive answer to the question: What is exceptional leadership, and how is it obtained? We need to journey ad fontes gubernatio—to the fountains of leadership—wherever we might find them.

Although we honestly look for answers to our leadership questions, the problem is that we are often not fully willing to embrace the change those answers might demand of us. Like the astronomers that followed Ptolomy's assertion, for fourteen hundred years, that the earth was the center of the universe, we naturally follow the momentum of ideas we are offered without questioning them foundationally; we do this often out of ignorance and other times out of plain laziness. Yet, a leadership renaissance rests in our desire for deep understanding and true change.

In their time, Copernicus, Galileo, and Kepler knew the dangers of opposing the Ptolemaic ideology. Still, they had discovered a source to new knowledge that instituted an innovative interpretation of the same sky that astronomers had been gazing at for generations. Despite the acrimonious response they received from their scientific colleagues and others in society, they stood up for what they observed and what they knew to be true. We have the great opportunity to examine leadership the same way. We should seek out and journey toward a leadership realm that is based on the willingness for reevaluation and reconstruction. We should no longer be satisfied with what we have inherited or the status quo.

We live in an era never before seen in history where leadership resources are vast and easy to obtain. In fact, the true scope of what is within our reach is rather staggering. The next time you are at a bookstore, take down one of the leadership books you see and imagine the following. On any given day, there are roughly 383,500 leadership-related books available through any one of the large online book distributors. Assume that each book is about one inch thick, and in your mind create a single column of all of those books stacked on top of each other. A balloon floating at 32,000 feet would miss this stack vertically by about fifty feet. This is an astounding picture to imagine—a stack of leadership resources six miles high. However, this collection of books doesn't include the thousands of articles written in professional and academic journals as well. So, as we stare skyward at this stack of knowledge, which leadership resource is the right one for our organization?

Finding a single and comprehensive source for leadership among them is clearly daunting. It would take several lifetimes to read all that is available to us and then extract the single truth that applies to our unique situation. This endeavor is hardly practical, so our solution is typically to read what we can, learn tactics from others, and make the best of our leadership roles through trial and error. We do what we can with what appears to work, and we call it leadership.

However, what if there were a better way? Rather than looking at the myriad of leadership models we build for unique circumstances, imagine if there were a way to change our leadership behavior from the inside—by examining what drives us at the core.

Step beneath the veneer of our pragmatism, consider what just works, and ask yourself the question: What really drives the possibility of achieving exceptional leadership? Where is its source? As we will find, the answer lies in the insights we can gain from objectively examining our instinctual behavior.

The ultimate goal in the chapters that follow is threefold. First, we need to find that which influences our behavior, evaluate what needs to change about these influences, and then make change happen. A renaissance of leadership is going to be more than just a mental exercise; it will be brought about by intentional transformation.

Untamed Leadership provides a pathway of thoughts and word pictures exploring the drivers of what makes us good and bad leaders. The journey is going to take us into many areas of discussion, but the main focus will be the examination of who we are in light of the raw instincts that contribute to what we do and how we think. These primal motivational forces, which were created in humans and animals, make up the source of complex behavior and all forms of leadership.

There is a kinship between humans and other cognitive animals through the common instincts we share. These are the untamed instincts. They are innate. They are there whether we think about them or not, and they will form the contours and substance of our actions with or without our consent. Think about this. We were born with instincts that shape our behavior. Left alone, these instincts will prime us to act and adapt to our environments unconsciously unless somehow modified.

We see this often in animals. For example, a newborn fawn already has the fight or flight instinct without ever observing that behavior from its mother. It knows how to lie close to the ground as still as a statue when it perceives a threat, and no one ever taught it to act this way. However, we can modify the fawn's flight instinct simply by feeding it routinely in our back-yards—which we shouldn't do. By conditioning its behavior with food, we can alter its instinctual response of seeing humans as a threat. We re-prime that fear instinct, and the fawn is less likely to run from us. Unfortunately, this means that the fawn is becoming less and less able to survive in the wild. We have desensitized it to natural and healthy forms of fear. Similarly, we do the same thing in our organizations. A new leader can walk in and change the dynamic of an entire organization simply by re-priming instinctual expectations engrained in the employees. Such a leader might do this intentionally or unintentionally—for the better or worse of the organization.

Still, there is a fascinating side to these instincts that is often overlooked. Even though humans have similar leadership instincts as animals, we haven't perfected them as well. What is amazing is that animals not only adhere to the innate instincts, but occasionally they show the ability to go beyond them and against them when they choose to do so. These animals are able to reshape or re-prime their untamed instincts for new and surprising behavior as required. They are capable of extraordinary behavior by cognitively choosing to go beyond what nature would otherwise dictate. Knowing this is apparent in the animal kingdom, what if we humans could do the same? What if we could step beyond ordinary leadership, acting as we have been programmed to function, and become reflective and adaptive—harnessing and stretching these instincts?

As you will discover along your journey in the following chapters, the answers to these questions is overwhelmingly positive. We have wonderful examples of successful leaders that harnessed and re-primed their instinctual behavior, often without knowing it, and ultimately experienced astonishing outcomes for those they led and their organizations as a whole. When these instincts are re-primed for exceptional leadership behavior, we find that our strategies will be more intrepid, our decisions will be more intuitively based on our understanding of those we lead, and we will be continually moving our teams and organizations into new realms of accomplishment.

We naturally have the choice to just let our lives play out these instincts without intervention, and the best we can hope for is to be mediocre leaders. The alternative is to step into a deeper understanding of who we are, why we behave the way we do, and develop a plan to reshape the leader inside us. With this in mind, we will be able to finally explain the sources behind innovative and valiant leaders like never before. We will have new tools that no one has ever used before to interpret leadership. And we will understand how to shape ourselves into people of substance and action for our organizations. Here within our untamed instincts we journey *ad fontes*—to the source of a leadership renaissance.

INTO THE WILD

Gary Larson illustrated it best with his *Far Side* comic depicting a student at the entrance of the "Midvale School for the Gifted." With all of his might and tenacity, this young prodigy strains to push the door of the school open with one hand while holding a pile of books in the other. His legs ache and his head is contorted downward in a herculean effort. Despite the boy's resolve, the door continues to resist. Yet, above his outstretched hand, which is pressed forcefully against the adversarial doorway, is a sign. The sign says "PULL."

One can't help but look at that scene with a bittersweet smile and think about the challenges we face as leaders. We know that we are capable of great things, and we want the opportunity to find significance in our organizations, our families, and in our own private lives. Still, try as we might, the doors that we think should fly open for us are few and far between. We exert massive amounts of force and yet feel we are going nowhere. We are weary from gauntlets of challenging situations and people. We toil against seemingly invisible forces and experience only few moments of epiphany as compensation for all of our efforts. We continue to push, when clearly the door says pull.

Untamed Leadership is about opening a door to the essential and elementary instincts that establish the way we interact with others—they determine the way we lead. We don't understand them very well, and we give them little attention. However, in the coming chapters, we will unveil them and examine the powerful and malleable force they have in our relationships and organizations. The evidence to their existence is overwhelming, and we are only beginning to understand the great benefits they offer in deciphering exceptional leadership ability. What we do know is that they are the fundamental components relied upon by all of the cognitive creatures of Earth.

Untamed Leadership uncovers the realm where we exert exceptional influence beyond what our mediocre predispositions for behavior might offer. It helps us examine our instincts and evaluate their impact on our lives and organizations. Through this discrete set of driving forces, we can shape the landscape of not only our own decisions but also of others around us.

Instincts form all kinds of behavior. We see them in a baby that is just born, in the soldier that gives his life to save his platoon, and in a missionary ministering to the emotional and spiritual needs of a family. In the animal kingdom, we see them in the behavior of pods of whales communicating over thousands of miles of open ocean and in the elephant mother nurturing its calf. We see similar instincts in staff meetings, hear them over the phone, and can experience them in nearly every social interaction. Our instincts are there nearly every social interaction. Our instincts are there when we exert authority and when we intently follow others. They act as the bedrock of leadership behavior for both humans and animals. As we study their role in our lives, we will realize how they establish who we are and why we behave the way we do.

Despite our vast resources and fortunate status at the pinnacle of the food chain, we as humans have much to learn about how leadership instincts work from animal societies. The similarities between the cognitive strategies of animal leadership and human leadership are uncanny. Yet, we are clearly the creatures who often need to catch up. The kinship we share is profound, and our increased understanding of animal behavior can only make us better people.

Sometimes our conclusions will be validated by what we see in the animal kingdom. Other times, we will stand corrected. For this valuable comparative feedback, we should be grateful as well as responsible stewards of the animals who inhabit our planet. Additionally, as easily as we study animals in the wild, we should be able to study ourselves. For within the depths of our psyches are resources that shape the contours of our leadership landscape, and we have a responsibility to the people we lead to take this seriously.

As we take the next step and journey to the core of untamed leadership, let us not forget that we are seeking a rebirth from the ideological constraints that have kept us from thinking clearly about who we are and our capabilities to prosper beyond current limits.

Untamed at the Core

Close to my home in the Rocky Mountains is a wolf sanctuary. At this rustic retreat among thousands of lodge pole pines, experts in animal care, veterinary medicine, and animal behavior extract wolves from around the country who have been abused and wounded, intentionally or by accident, and attempt to nurse them back to mental and physical health. Not all of the wolves survive the misfortune or brutality they experience. However, the ones who can overcome their obstacles often become permanent guests of these centers and live out the rest of their lives under the tender care of humans.[1]

Like any other canine, the wolf is an intelligent creature, but what sets it apart from others is its well-developed instincts and pack mentality. The wolf pack is more than just a simple hierarchy of animals. It is a collective intelligence. It is an adaptive system that harnesses the abilities and tactics of every member as efficiently as an elite Special Forces unit. The pack hunts, raises young, promotes and demotes leadership, manages internal corruption, punishes criminals, honors heroes, and nurtures an underlying structure of social cohesion. Packs are not necessarily families, although some of the members may be genetically related. They can be as small as a few members, or, in the case of Yellowstone's Druid pack, the largest and most researched pack ever documented, the size could be more than forty (although it has now been entirely decimated mostly through disease and competition for resources).[2] Whether as a small set of couples or dozens organized into a formal hierarchy, wolves work together using collaborative and adaptive behavior.

The ability for a single wolf to take on a leadership role rests within the pack rather than on the individual, and their management hierarchy is not as flat as we would think. In a pack there are typically four levels of membership: alpha, beta, subordinate, and omega. The alpha male wolf, while at the apex of molding the pack's behavior, is most commonly part of an alpha pair made up of a male and a female. The male alpha is the patriarch of the pack, and his mate manages the other females as the pack's matriarch. Next in line is the beta pair (or middle management). The rest of the pack is called the subordinates. And last is the position that no one ever wants.

They are called the omegas and represent the timid, defiant, and unpopular wolves that often find themselves ousted from a pack. They can expect to be picked on constantly and are usually the last to eat or find a suitable mate. When we talk about lone wolves, many times we are speaking of the omegas because of their inability to connect deeply to a pack's social structure. So, be careful calling someone a lone wolf—it isn't always a position to be admired. Also, the omegas typically are given this name because they exhibit behavior that is not conducive to the rest of the pack. They don't nurture relationships or care for others very well, and they don't acquiesce to the well-developed leadership ability of the pack's alpha. If they are able to survive for very long, they do it on their own roaming from pack to pack.

Alternatively, the alpha male is not just a slothful lord served by his peasants and common folk. He is an active participant in his individual and group instincts. As a result, he becomes president, chief hunter, director of homeland security, four-star general of the military, drill sergeant, and father figure to the pack. He provides the strategy and queues that enable the hunting pack to take down a seven-hundred pound elk at a full run. The bite strength of an average wolf is more than twice that of the average one-hundred-pound dog. However, bite is completely useless without a winning strategy—and this is where the alpha shines. For example, as a bull elk rounds a small hilltop of aspen trees, the alpha might signal the beta male to split the subordinates into two tactical teams. One group heads around the low side of a hill to the left, and the other, led by the alpha, drives up through the low brush on the right. As both teams round opposite sides, a quick howl announces that the elk has turned to the right, and the beta team kicks their run into high gear to blockade the naive bull against the other team's line of sharp, white teeth. It is this type of brainpower in an alpha pair that separate them intellectually from the rest.

One cool fall day, I spent several hours with the center's director watching a small pack interact. On this occasion, I sat inside the enclosure with the wolves. Occasionally, one of the friendlier subordinates would walk up and lick my mouth while pressing his giant white canines against the flesh of my face. This is the way that an outsider gets initiated into the pack—by a wolf kiss. Most of the time they lie on the ground pawing at visitors' hands to scratch their bellies. However, there were moments where a couple of wolves would have a brief teeth-showing tussle within a few feet of where I was sitting. These moments are short (perhaps only a few seconds), but can flood your bloodstream with adrenaline. Thankfully, in the pack I was observing, I was happily nothing more than a friendly distraction.

As I looked around, off in the corner of the large, natural enclosure sat a stalwart male. He was alone for the moment. He was the alpha male—the alpha among alphas. Although he clearly outweighed the others, his body mass was not what put him high in the leadership chain. This wolf had superior intelligence, intuition, and a guarded benevolence to those in the pack. His eyes were mighty—almost the size of a human's—and glistened golden in the morning sun. He sat with the regal posture one would expect from an alpha male. As the other wolves carried on playfully, he seemed to be watching them, but not as a mere observer. He was surveying his domain.

I sat in the dirt about twenty yards from where he had captured the shadow of a large pine tree. With a research notebook in my lap and camera around my neck, I documented his various glances and how the others perceived each queue. It wasn't until he caught me staring at him that I got a little nervous. It was the same kind of experience you encounter when people-watching and you catch the eye of someone else doing the same thing. However, it is a rare and rather uncomfortable event to catch the eye of a predator capable of running forty-five miles per hour.

As I sat there, I forcibly reminded myself that there were no known documented cases of unprovoked fatal attacks on humans in the lower forty-eight states. Still, I could not help but offer some sense of respect to this one-hundred-forty pound creature. Not only was he looking at me, but he also seemed to be reading the signals I was broadcasting—discomfort, mild anxiety, etc. I reclined my seated position in the dirt to emulate a submissive, subordinate pack member. After about five minutes, he got up from his matted-down grass, stretched, and started a slow walk—in my direction. That is when things got interesting.

I knew to pay close attention to the immediate behavior and reactions of the pack, and not necessarily the alpha's subtle posture and walking gait to understand his mood. When an alpha male is calm, the pack is calm. When he is on edge, the pack reacts as if on high alert. Unfortunately, the other four wolves in the enclosure were behind me and provided little visual assistance as to what was about to happen. By the time he cleared half of the distance to me, I had already stowed my camera and folded my notebook like I was preparing to go somewhere. The director of the center sitting nearby gave me a smirk like, "*Where do you think you're going?"* She was right. I could not outrun him nor hurdle the eight-foot fence behind me. So, I sat in the dirt at his mercy.

One of the problems with being adult humans is that we are deeply wired to primal instincts, and we are about as effective as infants at interpreting the best way to use them.

I looked down at the dirt, played with some grass near my foot, and acted as non-threatening and un-aware as possible. As he approached me, I slowly set out the last piece of a beef frankfurter and moved my hand to the ground about six inches from my leg. He sauntered up to me, sniffed my hand, delicately plucked the piece of meat, tossed it up in the air, and clamped his jaws together with nearly a ton of biting force. The sound jolted my ears, and I couldn't help but blink. He turned back to me, sniffed my shoulder, and licked the right side of my face. As he walked over to a patch of bright Colorado sunshine behind me, he lay down and closed his eyes. I took in a breath. One full minute later, my heart was still pounding like a bass drum.

This alpha wolf had no leadership certifications, no training conferences to attend, and no library of leadership books to read. Certainly, no consultant had ever offered him a better way to lead his pack. Every decision he made was trunked to ancient communica-tion lines of thousands of years of instincts. This wolf was a leader because of something deep within his psyche and well beyond his control. Yet, his presence alone among the other wolves in the pen was enough to set him apart.

I stood up, patted a few eager wolves on their heads, and walked out of the enclosure. I turned and closed the double gate, and the alpha was standing there looking at me. As our eyes locked again, I thought how instincts shape so many parts of behavior whether we cognitively process what they are or not. As I tossed the alpha a few snacks I had left over in my bag, there was no doubt that this wolf was no exception. Leadership is not exempt from the effect of untamed instincts. In fact, the antithesis is true—leadership is entirely dependent on them.

What Science Tells Us About Instinct

We know from extensive neurological and psychological research that the structure and function of the mind is vastly complex. Humans, as well as other animal species, are not limited to having only one instinct. There are naturally many. Our brains have the ability to downshift into primitive modes, or instinctual responses, when higher cognitive processes would otherwise be slow or inadequate. Some primitive instincts like fight-or-flight have been traced to the amygdala, which is a small area of the brain responsible for responding to, among others, immediate threats. For example, the amygdala is the primitive authority that makes us leap into flight mode when we are watching a scary movie. Other mammals like horses and deer are notorious for this same ability. They instinctively know that sudden or loud movements represent a threat. Alternatively, it is the fight side of the fight-or-flight instinct that enables a soldier or a law enforcement officer to attack rather than retreat from a hostile environment. They train vigorously to modify their response to these forms of stimuli. They reconstruct fear into an engaging, rather than a retreating, force.

Instincts go beyond simple interpretations of fight-or-flight, however. For example, at birth a human infant already has the instincts to suckle, root, cry, and grasp. By the time the child reaches toddler age, parents don't need to teach the instinct of self-preservation or selfish behavior—it just happens. In the early adult years, we attempt to educate our teenagers to be in proper control of the feelings that silhouette a strong hormonal drive and the new awkward desire for intimacy. Then in our twenties and thirties, our instinctual behavior is focused mainly on our social infrastructure and making decisions of self-reliance. As we grow older, these instincts might shift to be more inclusive of our families as we seek to sustain them financially, spiritually, or emotionally. The key is that while these instincts might change in their specific roles or intensity of involvement in our lives, they never go away.

The Origin of Instinct

The word instinct made its entrance into Middle English in the fifteenth century as a transliteration from the Latin words *instinctus* or *instinguere*, which means "to incite or instigate." As mid-nineteenth-century human psychology began to mature, it didn't take more than a century before other explanations for instincts became apparent. Most behaviorists asserted that instincts were more than pre-programmed patterns of behavior, and they were more complex than one could study via the scientific method. These behavioral and social psychologists believed not only that certain instincts were innate, but they could also be modified, and ultimately re-primed. This is an important element to shaping leadership instincts—for as we learn about their disposition, we will see the need to change their trajectory of behavior.

The nineteenth century offered a deeper examination of the role of instincts and their ability to be modified. American psychologist and philosopher William James once said, "*Instinct is usually defined as the faculty of acting in such a way as to produce certain ends, without foresight of the ends, and without previous education in the performance.*"[3] Likewise, in the book *The Original Nature of Man*, E.L. Thorndike expanded on James by stating, "*When the response is more indefinite, the situation more complex, and the connection more modifiable, instinct becomes the custom term.*"[4] Even the early social psychologists were coming to the realization that instincts were core functions of behavior having the characteristics of being both innate and modifiable. In his text, social psychologist William McDougall states:

While it is doubtful whether the behaviour of any animal is wholly determined by instincts quite unmodified by experience, it is clear that all the higher animals learn in various and often considerable degrees to adapt their instinctive actions to peculiar circumstances; and in the long course of the development of each human mind, immensely greater complications of the instinctive processes are brought about, complications so great that they have obscured until recent years the essential likeness of the instinctive processes in men and animals.[5]

What these leading psychologists were attempting to qualify was that both humans and animals have established instincts for certain actions, yet these instincts are capable of being changed through intention or circumstance. This is an important scientific discovery in that it explains the relationship between why we act a certain way and still have the ability to change how we act. No matter what we do now, we can change. Essentially, we are creatures bent toward a certain behavior at birth, we bend farther in different directions as our environment and choices influence us through life, and despite all of that—we are still able to change at any point. But how do these modifiable instincts relate to our behavior? The answer is found in how our brains respond to needs.

Instincts and Needs

In 1943, American psychologist Abraham Maslow offered a paper that classified five categories of human needs: physiological, safety, love/belonging, esteem, and self-actualization.[6] This layered approach is quite helpful when we look at the brain in terms of instinct and behavior because instincts respond to needs, and needs respond to instincts. To qualify how this works, we can imagine that a lower level need, such as a physiological need for food, would stimulate a lower level instinct in the limbic interior of the brain, such as hunting, to enable us to respond to that need. So we hunt because we need to eat. Similarly, as we look at the complexities of social behavior, we can see why social instincts are tightly linked to the social needs that we have. We build social communities because they benefit us and we provide benefits to them. One exists because of the other.

Not only do we establish the function of these instincts in relation to a specific need in the brain, but we also differentiate instincts from learned behavior by the speed at which information flows in the brain. For example, in 2008, scientists from Oxford University's Department of Psychiatry published a paper suggesting a possible basis for a parental instinct.[7] They observed a region of a mother's brain called the medial orbitofrontal cortex, located just over the eyes, which responds rapidly to the faces of infants but not adults. One of the researchers, Dr. Morten Kirngelbach, stated, *"These responses are almost certainly too fast to be consciously controlled and so are probably instinctive."* It is these fast responses in the brain that indicate the predisposition or presence of instinctual behavior. They do not necessarily exist at the base level reactionary area of our minds nor are solely within the high-level cognitive processing areas either. They exist in a functional area between the two. This layer is also where we find the seven untamed instincts. While they hide from our typical conscious minds, they are not invisible. They tie our instinctual reactions to dispositions of higher behavior. And because of this, they can be laid bare for our evaluation. To keep this idea in context, let's look at the following story.

Making Sense of Hikers and Mountain Lions

Three hikers were walking in a forest one late afternoon. As they rounded a turn, they froze in utter horror. Three large mountain lions were standing on the same path staring at them with their large teeth shining like white daggers. The first hiker shrieked instantly, turned around, and ran as fast as he could back down the path from where they came, and the first mountain lion instantly gave chase. The second hiker thought for a minute, pulled out a field guide on mountain wildlife, squatted down to appear less threatening, and started reading the book in a calm voice, attempting to soothe the savage beast. The second mountain lion looked at him for a few seconds and then lunged at him. The final mountain lion stared down the third hiker. The hiker thought, "*I can do what my gut says—try and run from this hungry animal, I can do what my head says—try and rationalize with this hungry animal, or I can go against my natural inclinations in both cases and try something different. I can respect the animal*

23

and my own survival at the same time." The hiker instantly grabbed the bottom of his jacket, lifted it high over his head, and with a strong voice said, "*GO AWAY MOUNTAIN LION, GO AWAY. I AM BIGGER THAN YOU!*" He said this again and again, and each time he stood a little higher on his tiptoes and spread his jacket out farther and farther—each time looking larger and larger. After only a minute, the final mountain lion turned and scampered quickly back into the forest.

The third hiker's mindset illustrates how to properly look at leadership instincts. We cannot be merely reactionary, responding to simplistic primed behavior, as the first hiker discovered. Neither can we intellectualize everything we do, assuming that through an academic mindset we can come to great power, as the second hiker discovered. Instead, we must understand how to harness our instincts for what they are, knowing that we can change them. The entire concept of who we are as leaders is dependent on how well we can accomplish this development effort.

After driving back from the Wolf and Wildlife Center, I spent the rest of the afternoon on my back porch contemplating these instincts while a small herd of deer grazed in a field behind my house. Nature had already figured out that untamed instincts are the apex forces that unite behavior. They can be witnessed in the self-preservation instinct of a pod of whales risking their lives to save a harpooned member of their family. They are found within the complexity of mimicry behavior exhibited by the cuttlefish. They traverse thousands of miles of open ocean through the communication instinct embedded in the grey whale. They enable the primate to process causality. Through the instinct of rationality, the dolphin has the ability to interpret the behavior of other species including humans. An instinct of duty nurtures and sustains the hierarchy that makes the wolf pack possible. And the elephant expresses what can only be interpreted as hope in the midst of despair and tragedy on the African plain. These same untamed instincts exist in all of us. They shape the way our social networks function and are the sources by which we lead and follow.

Over the course of the next few chapters, we will examine each instinct from several different perspectives. First, we will see the reality of each one in the animal kingdom and observe the remarkable behavior exhibited when animals transcend these raw innate forces. Next, we will see the human dimension from how each instinct plays an important role in our survival. Additionally, we will look at examples of both deplorable (omega) leadership and exemplary (alpha) leadership as a means to witness the polarity of human behavior. Finally, we will look at the instinct in action and ponder its relevance in our lives. We need to understand who we are from an entirely new perspective—a perspective relatively unknown to us until now. 🐾

1. SELF-PRESERVATION

"Among the natural rights of the colonists are these: first, the right to life; secondly, to liberty; thirdly, to property; together with the right to support and defend them in the best manner they can. Those are evident branches of, rather than deductions from, the duty of self-preservation, commonly called the first law of nature."
— *Samuel Adams*

"Our pleasures were simple; they included survival."
— *Dwight D. Eisenhower*

Because of one innate force, we all seek to survive. It is called the instinct of self-preservation. Consider that a majority of decisions we make in life will be comprised of choices for survival. Although seemingly obvious, the instinct of self-preservation is a complex interconnected process that consumes our brains every day. We are constantly evaluating threats to our physical survival, threats to the quality of the relationships we desire, threats to our comfort, threats to our resources, and threats to what or who is entrusted to our care. At a broader scale, this is the same source that shapes national ideologies, government legislation, political science, and has a profound influence on why wars are waged. It is the basis for which all living things function. Essentially, we are always trying to protect something—mostly ourselves.

27

Like the other instincts we will cover in this book, the instinct of self-preservation is relatively hidden from our day-to-day awareness even though it is the lens by which we look at everything, including leadership. Self-preservation will only reveal itself when provoked. For example, suppose that a car in front of you locks up its brakes with a loud screech. As your bloodstream is flooded with adrenaline, your brain reacts with physiological responses to provide you the most rapid response to avoid an accident. To the best of your body's ability, you are now working off of low-level survivability responses. As the milliseconds tick by, no other topic you have being mulling over—the grocery list, the projects on your desk at work, concerns about your teenage son's grades—matter at all. In fact, your brain reroutes your cognitive processing ability to functions that provide the best options for immediate survival. It is not until you fully recover from this experience that your brain returns you to more mundane thoughts and less immediate threats. These moments of seeing our lives pass before our eyes temporarily clue us into our raw requirement for survival.

Many events can trigger the self-preservation instinct. Your friend gets a disturbing call from her doctor while you are having coffee. The shock of unexpected news wipes the smile from her face. Your boss knocks on your door and says there is no other choice but to lay off twenty percent of the company's workforce. The master sergeant runs into your tent and says,

"Gear up, we're under attack." There is no avoiding it— the stimuli that initiate self-preservation responses are all around us in every environment, and we attempt to process them as they invade our self-built fortresses of humanity.

Beyond Mere Animal Instinct

Conceptually, we can interpret how the instinct of self-preservation works in a simple three-step process. First, we observe (or are stimulated by) a threat— no matter its intensity. Second, we process the threat through self-preservation dispositions. Finally, we respond to the threat. Although we can assume that the observation and response portions of this process are clearly important, what is most crucial in survivability is the second step—the examination of dispositions. A disposition means nothing more than our bent for certain behavior. They exclusively determine why we do what we do, and they are evident in every one of the instincts we will discuss.

Dispositions are shaped and reshaped over time by the repetition of old experiences and old behavior. They are also shaped and reshaped by the injection of new experiences and new threats. Our dispositions are hardwired into how we react to situations, and they rarely traverse the intellectual processing areas of the brain. These dispositions of instinct are the areas of our minds that prime us for certain behavior, and they are the portals from which we can view the inner construction of our instinct of self-preservation.

One of the best ways to examine dispositions is to examine them in their raw form—within the realm of the animal kingdom. For example, in 2009, National Geographic producers filmed a two-week-old African elephant baby whose family was frantically trying to get it to its feet. They sensed danger in the area, and the herd was on the move.[1] However, no matter what they tried, the youngling was too unstable and weak to join its mother and aunts in a desperate escape to safety. Despite multiple attempts by his relatives to lift him off the ground, the family quickly ran out of options. In order to protect the rest of the herd, they abandoned the baby elephant.

For over a day, the orphan stumbled on its weak legs alone through the grasses of Africa. What it didn't know was that something had picked up its scent and was closing in quickly. A pride of lions had been tracking the newborn for some time, and the chance for an easy meal was irresistible. As seven lions came into view, they targeted the baby and stalked it until they were in a position to strike. As they moved in for the kill, out of the bush came a thunderous crash. Bounding through branches and nearby trees, a massive bull elephant charged onto the scene with its ears spread like barn doors. The colossal male assailed the pride in a show of dominance and aggression. Over and over he pushed them farther and farther away from the baby. Despite the odds against him, he was able to fend off the pride's attack plans, and the lions quickly scattered. For the moment, the newborn was safe.

Nonetheless, animal behaviorists typically agree that bulls rarely engage in nurturing behavior, and the likelihood of this male staying with the baby elephant seemed unlikely. The filmmakers continued to follow the pair to see what would happen next. In a dramatic moment that was captured on film, the male began to gently touch the baby with its large trunk as if to communicate there was nothing to fear. Over a very short period of time, the bull began to endear the toddler as they walked slowly together, and they appeared to become companions. As they disappeared into the brush together and continued to meander across the dry plain, it is difficult not to hope that they continued to travel together for a long time.

This heartwarming story represents an instinctual anomaly. In an elephant herd, the females are in charge of the matriarchal society. Most of the time, bulls simply travel alone or in small bachelor groups apart from the females and the young. However, something changed this bull's mind and thus his instinctual behavior. He could have easily departed the area like the rest of the herd who put their own self-preservation above that of the baby. Instead, he went beyond the primal instinct of flight and extended his own sense of preservation to the younger and weaker one. Unlike the rest of the herd, the bull considered the preservation of this young elephant as seemingly more important than his own.

In another situation thousands of miles away, two young Indian elephant calves had gotten their feet lodged in between railroad ties on a set of train tracks in the forests of Bengal, India.[2] Their older relatives saw what had happened and worked diligently to dislodge their feet from the tracks. Nothing they did was working. As a roaring train approached, five adult elephants crowded closely around the calves in order to shield them from certain death. The railroad authorities were asked numerous times to not run trains through the forests at night or find alternate paths to avoid the likelihood of animal deaths. However, as Animesh Basu, president of the Himalayan Nature and Adventure Foundation reported, "*The drivers hardly ever adhere to the restrictions.*" The tragedy of trains killing elephants is not as rare as we would like to think, and many are avoidable. Still, any adult elephant who traveled this region in their lifetime would have witnessed or heard of the outcome of an animal versus the iron beasts that passed through the night.

On this dark evening, as the speeding train's headlights shined brighter and brighter against the backs of the adults huddled around their young on the tracks, their final moments were spent standing in opposition to their instinct of self-preservation. They defied their own sense of survival and attempted to protect the ones who were helpless. Having likely seen their relatives lying on the side of railroad tracks over the years, we can only surmise that their decision to put themselves in harm's way did not occur without the instantaneous flashes of images knowing what their decision would mean to their own existence. These adults surrendered their own self-preservation instinct to provide a chance for the survival of their young.

Across another ocean sat Binti Jua. She was a female lowland gorilla at the Brookfield Zoo in Illinois.[3] One afternoon a young boy climbed the wall around the gorilla enclosure, lost his footing, and fell twenty feet onto hard concrete. He was unconscious, and several limbs appeared to be twisted or broken. Seeing something drop into the enclosure, Binti Jua jumped off of her perch and made her way over to the boy while hooting deeply and loudly as an alarm. The boy's family and onlookers were wrenched in fear as they watched helplessly from above. With no way to intervene, his survival was entirely in the hands of a spooked female gorilla. However, of all the cages for this boy to fall into, few realized how important it was that he would fall into this one. Binti Jua happened to be the niece of the world famous Koko—who is well known for her amazing intellectual capacity as well as her ability to communicate via sign language. Still unconscious, the three-year-old boy didn't respond when Binti touched him gently. She poked the boy again. No response. While Binti continued to be curious, onlookers were frantically seeking help running all over the zoo. Still, there was no way to get an immediate response to the situation.

The other gorillas in the enclosure were disturbed by this intruder and started to make their way over to the boy. In a frightening moment that caused onlookers to gasp, a larger female rapidly approached him. Helpless as to what was about to happen, the boy's parents screamed. The female kept getting closer and closer, and then Binti made a decision. She went against the instinctual response that was driving all of the other curious and agitated gorillas in the enclosure. She intervened on the boy's behalf. With flared nostrils she growled until the other gorilla stopped closing in, and she continued to show her dominance until it retreated. Sensing that the boy was not going to be safe for much longer in his current location, she did something remarkable. With her own seventeen-month-old baby clutched to her back at the time, Binti gently picked up the three-year-old boy with one arm and cradled him briefly. Then she carried him over sixty feet to an access door where zoo personnel could reach him. He was rushed to the hospital and fully recovered a few days later. Binti Jua was considered a hero.

On the other side of the planet in frigid Pacific water, Marine biologist Ken Norris documented a case of selfless preservation within a pod of pilot whales. In this example, the pod had witnessed the harpooning of one of the members and quickly swam to its aid.[4] Two pilot whales quickly swam underneath and upward so that the fatally injured whale could breathe as it was being winched toward the collection ship. As it approached the stern, the pilot whale's comrades began doing something remarkable. They changed their response to the situation collectively. Instead of lifting the head of the whale from below, both of them began riding on top of the harpooned whale, pushing it down into the water. Contrary to the preprogrammed behavior of keeping a distressed whale on the surface, Norris suggested that the companion whales realized that it was more important to keep the wounded pilot whale out of the boat and in the water. Whether they realized the enormous amount of risk of being harpooned that they were putting on their own lives is something we can only guess. The whales responded instinctively to the initial problem. However, when the situation escalated beyond what they would normally experience (i.e. a whale exiting the water onto a boat), then a stronger and counterintuitive cognitive response resulted. These pilot whales had modified their instinct of preservation.

As we can see by these four stories of animal behavior, there is an underlying instinct of self-preservation governing our survival. However, these animals behaved in extraordinary ways. Each of them, as leaders amongst their peers, went against not only the expected behavior exhibited by others of their species, but also against their own internal dispositions for survival. They altered their disposition of self-preservation and imputed their own survival to others.

The Human Dimension: Self-Preservation

You won't find imputation covered in very many leadership courses, but it is a critical component to long-term organizational sustainability. It is the conscious, selfless actions we take to mutate egocentrism into altruism—from ourselves to others. It is the act of assigning a characteristic of survivability to someone who has no recourse or no volitional ability to do the same on their own behalf. The idea of imputing self-preservation shouldn't be an abstract concept. It simply means that leadership is an inclusive activity, and it becomes inclusive as we assign value and importance to others. As leaders, we protect what we value. Subconsciously, we look out for ourselves, but through conscious reevaluations, we modify the disposition of our self-preservation instinct and impute our survival onto others in the organization. This creates a sense of community within organizations and a shared interest where aspirations for survival coalesce as a collective. It also creates a leader who is in tune with the needs of his or her followers.

Self-preservation decisions are constantly reflecting this pre-primed concept of how to survive. Sometimes we make the decision to take flight. We forsake one of our own, emotionally or physically, because we have the perception that the only option for survival requires abandonment, just as the elephant herd exhibited abandoning their calf. Other times, we fight. We choose to become the bull elephant drawing a line in the sand regardless of cost and exclaim, "You shall not pass." Similarly, we might intervene as an advocate in another's helpless condition like Binti Jua or the whale pod. Still, there are times when we merely show solidarity. No matter the fierceness of a train roaring down the track, we encircle those who matter most to us knowing that we're all going down together.

How we behave in the face of self-preservation is largely determined by our instinct and ability to change the disposition of it. The choice is ours. Think back to the roles of wolves within the wolf pack. Among the layers of the hierarchy, there are the dominant alpha wolves and the weaker omegas. By examining those roles, the choices we have become obvious. We can take an active role in the shaping of our instincts and our future (the alpha), or we can take a passive role leaving our future up to how our instincts are shaped by the dysfunctions of our environment (the omega). Either we choose to be an alpha wolf working diligently to lead our behavior, or we succumb to the destiny of the omega who follows where our behavior leads us. In our culture, we see many examples of alphas and omegas. Let's first take a look at omega behavior.

The Omega of Self-Preservation

The news media is a great resource for showing the variety of ways that humans are polarized regarding survival instincts. Consider the headlines and imagine putting an 'E' next to every story where the protagonist made egocentric decisions with respect to self-preservation. One afternoon I read the following 'E' headlines: "Insurgents coordinate strikes against 13 cities in Iraq; Attack on military computers confirmed; 'I've been Through Hell,' Tiger Woods' ex-wife says; HP CEO resigns after sex harassment investigation; Executive steps down for review of Apple kickback charges." Alternatively, consider doing this same news analysis but this time put an 'A' next to every story where an altruistic decision is made. On the same news website, I found these stories: "*Sacrifice: An American Virtue on Rebound; Good Samaritan Saves Man on Metro Tracks; Dramatic Sea Rescue Caught on Tape; Leader Commits Company to Donate Time and Money to Multiple Charities; Gates Foundation Looks for Ways to Educate the World's Forgotten.*"

Although we dislike the consequences of 'E' behavior, there is no doubt we like to hear stories about it. Perhaps this is because it feels good to know that there are people out there worse off than we are. Nonetheless, the dark, egocentric side of self-preservation is unfortunately nothing surprising—it's popular. Just look at the most successful movies and television shows today: stories about greed, lust, murder, and corruption sell. Yet, the damage from organizations led by egocentric individuals is no longer casual news. Our own lives are now being directly impacted through job losses, economic downturn, investment failures, and so on. The corrupt lives of Ken Lay (Enron), Bernie Ebbers (WorldCom), John Rigas (Adelphia), Angelo Mozilo (Countrywide), and Bernie Madoff (of the largest Wall Street investment Ponzi scheme in history) have now become some of the most well-documented business and law case studies in U.S. history. And they have become our yardstick for sinister leader behavior.

In their book *Charting Corporate Corruption: Agency, Structure, and Escalation*, Peter Fleming and Stelios Zyglidopoulos write:

After viewing the secretly shot video of Andy Fastow, the Chief Financial Officer of the doomed Enron Corporation, one is left with the undeniable impression that this man is a 'bad apple'. In the grainy footage, he successfully convinces dimwitted bankers of the integrity of his shady business model. Indeed, given what we now know about the fraudulent nature of Fastow's Byzantine accounting methods, Fastow himself comes across as a scoundrel with few scruples about the harm he was causing others. Moreover, as Fastow fools his audience and manipulates the figures in such a brazen fashion, the physicality of the man himself exudes badness, a kind of devilish spark reminiscent of the protagonist in the film American Psycho: handsome, intelligent and assertive, yet devious, wily and patently dangerous. We get the same feeling when Fastow later takes the stand during his court appearance before receiving a six-year prison term. His discourse and demeanour betray the figure of a Machiavellian schemer who would not think twice about wrecking the company in order to make more money.[5]

Analyzing the situation a little more rationally, we can deduce that Fastow's behavior is not something he turned on one afternoon when he decided corruption would be the best method for obtaining easy money. Rather than being a single choice, omega behavior is reinforced over time. A corrupt mind is sculpted—

through small hits of a chisel. An omega-focused leader validates his disposition and justifies its existence. Done enough times, these leaders are no longer able to remember a time when they didn't think this way. They have created a trap and are now caught in it.

Yet, every leader has the potential to be a benevolent and egalitarian power within their organization. They equally have the same potential to be a ruthless, self-aggrandizing, megalomaniacal force. But what decisions do we make to establish this proclivity? It starts with a view of who needs preserving. As a leader, we will have the natural desire to preserve someone. We will make decisions that are always influenced by the idea that we are preserving or protecting a certain person, group, thing, ideology, etc. For example, the reason why a good father would not let his young children run aimlessly through a crowded public place is because his idea of self-preservation includes the protection of his family. He has imputed his concept of preservation to them. The father's fundamental self-preservation instinct has been altered so that he is not just aware of threats to himself but equally to his children.

For an omega leader, he or she will make decisions for the organization where there is always a personal benefit—consciously or subconsciously—even if it means greater risk to the organization. It doesn't take an Enron scandal or a $400,000 luxurious vacation only one week after the AIG multi-billion-dollar bailout by the U.S. government to make this concept clear.

Over the course of four years, I researched a small company. At the time, I was studying the relationship between oversight and corruption in leadership hierarchies. The executives were not power players by any means. With the average stock price between $2 and $5 over any given year, the executive leaders were salaried at well under $1 million each. There was no corporate jet, no chartered limousines, and from all outside appearances the executives ran a frugal business and lived relatively frugal lives. However, under the thin covering of a stable organization ran the dark rivers of secret alliances, executive greed, and corrupt practices.

Executives flew their family members first class on international business trips to exotic locations, staying at only five-star resorts, and charging the trips to the company. This did not just occur once; among the three top-level executives, this happened ten to twenty times per year. All disguised under a pseudo-executive privilege, these individuals carried out their personal vacations on the company tab. Expensive gifts, flowers, and other perks were constantly flowing out of the executive budgets. The executive staff administrators were well aware of the corruption but were too frightened to confront investors or board members with the truth. It seemed that the entire top layer of the organization was in the club.

At the same time, layoffs were the norm. Besides the greed emanating from these leaders of the organization, they were making unpredictable and seemingly careless decisions with staffing. For example, one year the entire marketing department of the company was laid off. This represented a massive loss of brain trust in the boutique products they produced. Sales quickly slumped, as did employee morale. Without any oversight, this group of omega leaders had built a company to finance their own lifestyles. Many within the organization felt trapped with few options to use their niche expertise. No one had imputed a sense of self-preservation to them.

Naturally, we look at the vacuum leaders like these create and we tend to say, "Well, I am nothing like them." However, we need to be vigilant in our own evaluation of self-preservation dispositions. Although only a small percentage of us might have the opportunity to become executive officers or general managers of an organization, there is no doubt that we all have the capability for omega behavior. Thus, it is necessary for us to evaluate where we are between egocentrism and altruism and make some very important choices based on the impact we are having and the example we are setting for others.

The Alpha of Self-Preservation

On the opposite side of the spectrum is the leader who has an alpha disposition for self-preservation. The alpha leader is concerned about others—imputing a self-preservation drive onto those within the organization. Rather than relying on the way they have always done things, the alpha consistently evaluates how their dispositions are bent: Are they more egocentric? Are they more altruistic?

When examining our self-preservation instinct, we are given two things: (1) the opportunity to see our current disposition of behavior; and, (2) the choice whether or not to change our instinctual course. From an alpha standpoint, this is done simply by looking to whom or what we impute our concept of self-preservation. For example, in British Prime Minister Tony Blair's memoir, he describes the distressing situation that prompted a Royal Air Force jet to tail a commercial airliner in preparation for firing upon it. He writes:

> "A passenger plane had been out of contact for some time, and was heading over London. I had the senior RAF commander [authorized] to get my decision. The fighter jet was airborne. For several anxious minutes we talked, trying desperately to get an instinct as to whether this was threat or mishap. The deadline came. I decided we should hold back. Moments later the plane regained contact. It had been a technical error. I needed to sit down and thank God after that one!"[6]

Prime Minister Blair's potential dilemma rested on the imputation of self-preservation to everyone in London and everyone on the plane at the same time. Had the events continued on for a few more minutes, the polarizing decision moment would have occurred: Do we shoot down this plane, now? Thankfully, that didn't happen. However, regardless of the outcome,

Mr. Blair's disposition had already been established. He had already imputed his instinct of self-preservation to everyone involved in this situation, and that underlying basis was the foundation that made him delay military action.

Whether an animal or a human, the choices that we make, and the underlying instinctual dispositions that support those choices, are primed toward self-preservation. We must ask ourselves—are we acting as alphas or omegas? We can only know this by observing the responses we have to situations today, processing why we have those responses, and then working to realign that disposition of behavior toward the goal of healthy outcomes. But how do we find a healthy outcome? To answer this, let's look at James Fields.

In late September 1944, U.S. Army First Lieutenant James Fields of the 10th Armored Infantry, 4th Armored Division was caught in a massive firefight with Nazi infantry that had entered the small French town of Rechicourt.[7] His platoon had few backup resources, and many of the troops were wounded. The mission that day was to counter the attack of the Nazis in the small town near Luxembourg and strike a blow to the opposition forces in that area of eastern France.

Fields saw a soldier in his platoon get wounded in an open area that left him vulnerable to another attack. With no apparent concern for his own welfare, Fields left the makeshift trench he occupied with several other soldiers and began providing first aid. Upon his return to the protection of the trench with the ailing soldier, a mortar shell exploded with fragments cutting through his face and rendering him unable to speak or yell out commands. As platoon leader he was seemingly helpless. However, to the astonishment of his fellow soldiers, Fields ignored his severe wounds and began leading his team using only hand signals. Shortly after being wounded, his unit came under crossfire between two enemy positions. His platoon's nearby machine gun post had been disabled and could provide no protection for the troops huddled down in a trench. Fields jumped from his protected position, ran to the light machine gun bunker, picked up the weapon, and began firing it by resting it on his hip. Without a cross hair sight to look through, Fields took out both flanking enemy positions.

The sight of First Lieutenant Fields singlehandedly taking on the enemy released an adrenaline rush in the remaining troops under his command, and they joined the fight. During the final moments of the battle, his unit harassed the enemy until they eventually retreated and scattered into the outlying countryside. Not only had Fields successfully completed his objective, but he had also bolstered the dedication and duty of his men that day.

As a result, General George Patton, Jr. field promoted First Lieutenant Fields to Captain and recommended him for the Congressional Medal of Honor. Patton then sent him home and later mentioned in the book *War As I Knew It* that he didn't want "*Lieutenant Fields sent to the front any more, because it has been my unfortunate observation that whenever a man gets the Medal of Honor or even the Distinguished Service Cross, he usually attempts to outdo himself and gets killed, whereas, in order to produce a virile race, such men should be kept alive.*" Nearly every Medal of Honor story reads like this where under exceptionally dire circumstances, a single or group of individuals exhibit an exceptional level of courage to overcome formidable odds. Yet, this concept of courage is not something of an achievement of valor alone, nor is it something that comes out of nowhere. It comes from a self-preservation disposition that is not inwardly facing. Rather than seeking ways to preserve our own survival, we embrace what must be done for others as well.

Since we know that the instinct of self-preservation is going to impact our leadership behavior, we need to know what it will do to others. Will the people we lead see someone who is looking out for their best interest like First Lieutenant Fields? Or will they see someone who misuses their trust? The only way to know this is by looking at how our disposition is set. Like checking a navigational bearing, we need to do this habitually.

During the Apollo 11 moon mission, the crew navigated to the moon by first querying a navigation computer that would display a calculated star location. With that data, one of the astronauts then took out a sextant and pointed it out a cabin window. The crew corrected the location data in the computer with the correct star location from the sextant, and the computer continued to plot a corrected path to the moon.

Despite the complex mathematical tables in what we would view as a rudimentary computer today, this system needed to be realigned in real-time by a secondary and more reliable source—objective reality. The crew made this modification over and over to keep the computer in alignment with the observable star field. In the same way, we shouldn't expect that our concept of self-preservation is accurate every day and in every situation. A correction process is needed not only to align us with our goals of being alpha leaders, but also to be able to routinely expose our assumptions about how we lead.

A theme to which I've adhered throughout life is AQA, which stands for *Always Question Assumptions.* It is critical for leaders to always derive our understanding of life from an ongoing critique, analysis, review, and synopsis of meaningful information about ourselves. This doesn't mean to be a perpetual pessimist. Instead, it represents a way of thinking that is always evaluating fact and truth in light of other fact and truth. AQA is the realignment tool we need to become alpha leaders.

Self-Preservation in Action

In mid-2001, David T. McLaughlin was appointed Chairman of the Board of the American Red Cross (AMC). He had an extensive background in leadership emanating from his years as a U.S. Air Force pilot, President of Dartmouth College, executive officer over Orion Safety, Toro Products, and Champion International. He sat on the boards of Viacom, ARCO, and Chase Manhattan Bank, and was the President and CEO of the Aspen Institute whose mission is to "foster values-based leadership, encouraging individuals to reflect on the ideals and ideas that define a good society, and to provide a neutral and balanced venue for discussing and acting on critical issues."[8]

What David did not know was how important his leadership disposition would be required on 9/11, three months after he took his office at AMC. He said, *"The events of 9/11 changed not only the way the Red Cross prepared to respond to weapons of mass destruction disasters, but also reinforced the need to work collaboratively with other agencies that either have more capability than we do or provide needed services that are not part of our mission."*[9] Amid the confusion of gathering and distributing resources, not to mention the allocation of funds, David led the organization through one of its most challenging periods. His leadership forged a path for self-preservation—via the effort and concern imputed by the executive staff for the mission of the AMC but also for the role of self-preservation that the AMC had for the victims of disasters like those of 9/11.

At the very foundation of the AMC ideology, David asserts, *"the organization had to reassess its chartered mission and to realign assets to respond to the challenges of an entirely new environment."* Without an alpha disposition for self-preservation, what David and his staff accomplished during this critical time in

U.S. history would not have been possible. There was no room for an omega. He will always be remembered for his role in sustaining the country during a time of great need. David passed away of natural causes in 2004 while on a fishing trip with his family.

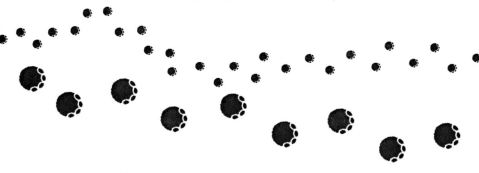

Our self-preservation instinct is a root force of behavior. Because of its influence on every part of our lives, it is a difficult thing to think about. It consists of examining the raw underbelly that motivates our decisions. Yet, it is an achievement that we all should strive for, and the vulnerability that it reveals should only promote an eagerness for change. This change is about balance. Like the fulcrum supporting a playground teeter-totter, any offset simply creates dysfunction. When we balance healthy actions of leadership with healthy thinking of leadership, then we have found an equilibrium that is now useful in our organizations. We should be spreading self-less preservation like a wildfire among our peers and followers—for it is through this cascading dedication to others that we revolutionize our workplaces, homes, communities, and societies.

Very few leaders take the time, which you just have, to examine how their concept of self-preservation is impacting their behavior and the other people in their organization. Consider that the mere exercise of thinking about this instinct has just brought you to a new level of awareness about how every organization operates. Perhaps you just modified your instinct by reading this chapter. ●

Principles for Reflection

- We all are subconsciously preserving someone or something.

- A majority of all leadership decisions we make contain components of self-preservation. Can you identify them?

- How we are primed or disposed to self-preservation behavior will determine how we project self-preservation into our organizations.

- Every self-preservation choice we make reinforces or contradicts our current behavior.

- We should always be aware of whom we impute our instinct of self-preservation to and why.

- Where is the dividing line between our self-preservation and what we impute to others? Would others be surprised to know where we draw the line?

2. MIMICRY

"No man, for any considerable period, can wear one face to himself, and another to the multitude, without finally getting bewildered as to which may be the true."
—Nathaniel Hawthorne

"Most people are other people. Their thoughts are someone else's opinions, their lives a mimicry, their passions a quotation."
—Oscar Wilde

Whether a teenager pining for expensive jeans her friends are wearing or a new employee trying to make a good impression in his first staff meeting, we all attempt to fit into social situations by watching and imitating others. We want to feel included, even if only by one other person, and to assist in making this possible, we subliminally observe others' behavior to help us clarify our own. As Gail T. Fairhurst asserts in her book *The Power of Framing: Creating the Language of Leadership,* "*We routinely mimic others' facial expressions, body language, speech patterns, and vocal tones in social interaction, and only sometimes are we aware of it.*"[1] What we do with mimicry is more than just an attempt to mirror others' behavior. In fact it is a complex collaborative effort of social negotiation. Our minds have a plan, and it is to establish an unconscious sense of belonging. And this belonging creates the survivability of a community. In this chapter, we examine mimicry and explain why leaders must be fully aware of the social impact this powerful instinct has on their behavior and of those in their organizations.

With any human interaction, there is a subliminal and instantaneous spark of association awareness. We use this awareness as the starting point to figure out how to connect. We extend our antenna to sense for commonality between others and ourselves, and we make assumptions based on the feedback we receive. We make subtle negotiations that continue back and forth in an ongoing effort to find a level of connectedness. And mimicry allows us to do this.

To better see how this instinctual layer of activity shapes our behavior, let's consider this simple example: Suppose that you are a tourist in a new city and realize you are lost. You walk toward a police officer to ask for directions to your hotel. In an instant, your mind is perceiving and interpreting the officer's non-verbal behavior such as his appearance, demeanor, facial expressions, body stance, and so on. With this limited information, you approach him. If the officer has a smile already on his face, you might subconsciously mimic that smile. If the officer has his arms folded with a stern look, you might mimic a more timid appearance in order to sway his willingness to help you.

From the officer's vantage point, he performs a similar analysis. Based on what he can observe about you externally, he has already evaluated whether you are a potential threat or not, someone in need of some assistance or not, or a person whom he can ignore. Like the nonverbal negotiation that you offer the policeman, he offers a negotiation in return—hopefully through a simple smile. Before you have said even one word, both of you have processed initial observations. And within seconds, you and the policeman have established a social exchange of connectedness. With that established, you are ready to make your request for directions, receive guidance from the officer, and be on your way.

What is most fascinating about this instinct of mimicry is that, like the self-preservation instinct, it stores certain dispositions. Let's expand on the policeman example for a moment. Suppose that as you walk away from the officer, you realize that you forgot to ask for the nearest pharmacy. You turn around and head back in his direction. As you approach the officer a second time, what happens? The negotiation time is much shorter. You already know each other—to an extent. With this in mind, you walk up to him and quickly ask for additional assistance. He answers quickly, and you head off in the right direction. Your disposition for mimicry had already been established from the first negotiation. You already knew what mimicry needed to be done, like echoing the smile on his face, to assist in getting the information you needed. This is the natural and positive side of mimicry behavior in social engagements. We mimic in order to better connect.

However, the idea of mimicry also stirs up negative connotations. The nightly news provides plenty of examples such as someone impersonating an officer of the law, trying to exaggerate credentials to get a job, or making false claims to earn a military medal. The dark side is certainly visible to us, but we have to understand that mimicry used as an inauthentic manipulation tactic is not the same as mimicry used for deeper connectedness or survival. Where the former might elicit dysfunctional behavior, the latter contributes to the depth and survivability of our social interactions. One of the best ways to look at the raw and perfected development ability of mimicry is by looking at animals. Although we all mimic differently in execution, the underlying purpose and function for it is often the same. We all just want to survive social encounters.

Beyond Mere Animal Instinct

Mimicry is best understood within the context of what it means to survive. For animals, sometimes this means that mimicry is a way to preserve a bloodline by finding a suitable mate. Other times mimicry is the visual or audible behavior that helps to connect creatures in a social environment. Still, it could just mean a way to fool a predator.

The variety of mimicry and pretending going on within the animal kingdom is about as diverse as in human behavior—but much more flamboyant. For example, a female killdeer bird has a well-documented behavior where it pretends to be hurt by struggling on the ground in a wing-dragging motion.[2] The bird is not injured. Instead, it makes itself vulnerable in order to lead a predator away from her nest. Once she feels the threat is at a safe distance, she flies away and eventually makes her way back to her eggs.

The eyed hawk moth has an interesting way to scare away predators. It has two sides to its wings. One side looks like a dry crumpled leaf. When a bird gets too close, the moth flips its wings over to display the underside, which is brightly colored and mimics the shape of hawk or owl eyes. The perception of large eyes scares away the bird.

Another fascinating example of mimicry behavior exists in the African pin-tailed whydah birds. The females intentionally lay their eggs elsewhere—in the nests of waxbill birds. Surprisingly, the waxbill females do not reject the additional eggs. In fact, they nurture them. As it turns out, the whydah juveniles imitate the same plumage and gape of their mouths as their hosts. The waxbill parents are unable to distinguish the whydah's from their own and raise them. In this way, the whydah birds continue their survival by using the resources of others.

Dr. Jurgen Nicola, first to study this behavior, brought home some young whydahs and didn't realize until they started to grow past the juvenile stage that two of his birds were actually waxbills.[3] They looked identical. From chameleons that change with the color of their surroundings, toads that defend themselves by inhaling air that makes them three to four times their size, the African cutthroat finch that hisses and wiggles its body like a snake when it is threatened, to the decorator crab that disguises itself by gluing seaweed to its body, nature uses mimicry and pretending for all forms of survival.

Eugene Linden, animal behavior journalist, observed the importance of mimicry and pretending and the role of survival in humans and animals. In Linden's research, the role of this behavior actually took on greater complexity in how it was accomplished and for what apparent purpose:

> *Huge numbers of creatures practice deception, but most don't know that they do it. The leafy sea dragon from southwest Australia is a sea horse that looks for all the world like a floating bit of seaweed. It's a clever disguise, since the creatures that eat sea horses typically don't eat floating seaweed, and the creatures that eat floating seaweed are not interested in eating leafy sea dragons . . . The leafy sea dragon probably does not know that it looks like a piece of seaweed. Sometime in the distant past a chance mutation left some ancestral sea horse with a feathery appendage that confused enough predators so that those sea horses with such accoutrements had a better chance to survive and breed. . . Then there are deceptions rooted in behavior—where an animal does appear to invent a deception, as, for instance, when a dog limps to get petted, the reasoning might simply be: "If I do this, he'll do that," rather than, "If I can convince the boss I'm hurt, he'll be nicer to me."*

Then there are cases that involve the conscious planting of a false belief. During World War II, the Allies let the Germans discover a body they had planted off the coast of Spain. Among the dead man's belongings was a briefcase carrying "secret" messages suggesting that the Allies planned to launch their invasion of Europe in Greece. The reasoning behind this was that the Germans were more likely to believe this disinformation if they had to work to disguise and interpret the messages themselves.[4]

While many modes of mimicry occur in the nonverbal realm, as Linden portrays, there are also many examples that use verbal or audible mimicry. As we can expect, birds have taken the tool of audible impersonation to grand extremes.

For example, the mockingbird, in Latin called *Mimus Polyglottos* (for many-throated mimic), has a unique characteristic not often found in other birds of the family of mimic thrushes. It can mimic sounds besides those of other birds. It is not uncommon for a mockingbird to imitate animals like squirrels and small dogs, a rusted gate swinging in the wind, the brakes of a car driving by, or even insects.[5] Adults can keep a collection of dozens of songs and vocalize them from memory. They might learn new sounds once and not sing them again for months.

Mockingbirds can adapt songs into new variations while still retaining the perfect pitch and pronunciation of the original song they learned. They are ambient sound artists because of the necessity for survival.

As ornithologists researched the vocal complexities of mockingbirds, they revealed that the repertoire of tunes produced by the males helped to attract particular females. The more they practiced the songs, the better the males got at singing. Females picked up on the subtle accuracy and inaccuracy in the songs, and they could determine which male was the most mature of the singers they were hearing. Simply by singing a song that was collected and imitated from another source, a strong male could find a strong female and preserve their genetic line.

Sometimes the goal of survival is not just about long-term strategies of genealogical sustainability. Instead, it is all about immediate threats. For the cuttlefish, a close relative to the octopus and squid, the challenge of survival is much more personal. Keri Langridge and colleagues from the University of Sussex observed that these intelligent invertebrates can target their defensive responses to the hunting capabilities of different predators.[6] What is more remarkable is that it is clearly innate behavior. The young cuttlefish used in tests had never been educated in the wild. They just simply knew how to identify and uniquely respond via mimicry to each type of predator.

In the tests, three very different predators approached the cuttlefish: young seabass, dogfish sharks, and crabs. They were separated from their hunters via a protective glass partition in the aquarium. One of the remarkable capabilities of a cuttlefish is its ability to create dynamic, hypnotic displays on its skin. Like synchronized and rhythmic variations of color and shape, it can mimic the colors of other fish, morph to shapes of coral indigenous to a reef, or blend with flickering sunlight reflecting through the dust and debris in the water. Its skin has the ability to not only emulate its visual surroundings but also make itself into an artist's canvas as it paints visual stimuli that it uses for hunting, courting a mate, and defending itself.

In what initially appeared to be a puzzling response, Langridge found that the cuttlefish only used their range of dynamic visual patterns when they were in proximity to a seabass. The answer to this puzzle made perfect sense. Seabass hunt visually. The cuttlefish flattened their bodies to look proportionally larger and displayed two dark spots on their backs that were disconcerting enough to the seabass that it swam away nearly every time.

However, when the predator was a crab or a dogfish, the cuttlefish never responded with any visual indicators. The reason that it didn't emulate the same behavior exhibited with the seabass was that crabs, as well as dogfish sharks, do not use vision to hunt. Crabs sense chemicals, and sharks sense electrical fields. In response to these predators, the cuttlefish just swam quickly away.

Based on its observations, the cuttlefish interpreted the threat and provided a specific survival response. It is still a mystery to many scientists how a creature shortly after birth could innately know the hunting capabilities of a predator it had never seen. Nonetheless, the instinct of mimicry and pretending are innately wired into this animal's survival responses.

In higher cognitive animals, survival behavior can also take on a much more community-related impact—a sense of belonging. In the Atlas Mountains of Algeria and Morocco live the Barbary macaque monkeys. While researching their maternal behaviors, Anne Zeller observed a female who was watching and considering the behavior of other females nursing their infants. Having no baby of her own, this female picked up and held her two-year-old sister as if it were an infant. Zeller states, *"[she] cuddled her, groomed her and provided visual cues to how her sister should feed."*[7] She did this in the same exact manner as the other females who had babies. From all appearances, the female monkey might have been pretending that she had a baby like the other females—just for the sake of pretending. Alternatively, it is certainly possible that as an attempt at connecting deeper with the other females in the troop from whom she felt excluded, she emulated their behavior—just like we would emulate the external nonverbal cues of a group of people we admired or wanted to join.

As complex creatures, we all use the instinct of mimicry for different purposes. Sometimes it is the defense mechanism that makes us invisible or more threatening to a would-be predator. Other times it is a way for us to impress others. And last, it is a social tool for enjoining us deeper to a group to which we want to belong. There is no doubt that the effects of mimicry and pretending can be observed in how we behave on a daily basis, often without our awareness. However, what impact does this instinct have on the human social realm? How does it shape the behavior of people in families, teams, and organizations? And how does it impact the role we have as leaders? To answer these questions we will now take a deeper look at the human dimension of this instinct.

The Human Dimension

We seldom examine the general role of mimicry in our own lives. Yet, as we have seen, this instinct is a critical area silently modifying our behavior. Like a Wizard of Oz, the instinct of mimicry pulls the levers and pushes the buttons controlling an impressive display of behavior all the while hiding behind a curtain of obscurity. Our goal here is to pull back that curtain and see what and why things happen. Renowned psychologist Jessica Lakin of Drew University produced a fascinating study that can help us look at this topic of innate, human mimicry in a new light.[8]

In her research, she questioned the essential structures and strategies that we use to affiliate ourselves into social groups. In order to look at this deeper, she decided to research the extremes of mimicry. What would happen if someone were threatened to be isolated socially? Would he or she mimic the behavior of a certain group in order to gain back acceptance? Lakin constructed a study such that volunteers played an online video game that apparently was networked to other volunteers. In reality, each of them was playing against a computer. As the game progressed, the computer selected certain players who would be included more in the game and others, less. Essentially as a form of football, the computer selected certain players to get the ball routinely, while others were left out. As expected, those that the computer left out felt somewhat ostracized from the group who received the ball over and over. Likening back to the mentality of a childhood playground, the researchers had quickly created a group of volunteers who felt included and a group who felt excluded.

Next, Lakin had each volunteer sit in a room by themselves and had cameras record their foot movements. As the volunteers sat alone, Lakin recorded of their foot behavior to establish baselines. After a period of time, a woman would enter the room to begin working with the volunteer on a shared project. This plan was also part of the research fabrication. The woman's real responsibility was to continually wiggle her foot back and forth while she and the volunteer worked together.

Surprisingly, these volunteers, who had previously felt rejected by the other players of the game, subliminally mimicked the foot behavior of the new woman in the room. Their feet began wiggling back and forth. Their instinct of mimicry was attempting to establish a connection with this new person who might make them feel included—potentially to offset the feeling of exclusion that occurred previously.

Additionally, the team conducted a new test where they changed the parameters of the game. This time they had only women play the game where the computer simulated their exclusion by both virtual men and virtual women players. As expected, the women volunteers all walked away feeling left out at the game's conclusion. Each of the women was then isolated in individual rooms, and their alone foot movements were recorded again. This time, the researchers tested whether the gender of the companion put into the room would impact the volunteer's foot movements. It did. Lakin observed that when a woman, as opposed to a man, was put into the room and started wiggling her foot, the rejected volunteer (also a woman) would wiggle her foot. Essentially, all of the women volunteers were making efforts to resolve disparity between themselves and the women that had seemingly excluded them in the game.

Lakin's work is helpful for our study of the instinct of mimicry because it shows how little we know about what drives the signals we are sending in our social environments. Like many other complex creatures, we simply do what we instinctively interpret to be the best behavior for maintaining what we consider to be community. We have intention behind these actions, even though we have no idea they are occurring. The role of intention is very important at this point because, like the volunteers seeking to reestablish connectedness, the need for inclusion in specific groups reveals the disposition of the instinct of mimicry. It tells us why we are acting the way we are. Sometimes this disposition produces positive mimicry behavior, and sometimes the alternative is also true.

The Omega of Mimicry

For the omega mimic, one who displays dysfunctional mimicry behavior, there are many ways in which this instinct can be counterproductive to healthy communities. For example, there are growing issues with exaggerated resumes and diploma mills in the corporate world. People misrepresent how they look on paper in order to gain a personal advantage that would otherwise not be provided to them. Also, we have seen increasing instances of individuals faking military service in order to gain notoriety and receive free or discounted services from the local community. Some have gone so far as to wear uniforms and participate in public ceremonies for service they never performed and attempt to use medals that they were never awarded. In 2005, the Stolen Valor Act made it a federal crime to verbally or in written form claim to have received any military award that had not been awarded.[9] We have even seen reports of people who claim to have received the Purple Heart, and when the investigation was completed, they went to jail.

For over a year, Colorado State Police tried to track down a police impersonator. He had dropped out of the local police academy due to poor performance, yet he still felt the desire to be a police officer—so much so that he obtained a red flashing light for his car, which happened to be a retired police cruiser. He started his own security company which had no clients, of course, and put a security emblem on his vehicle's front door panels that looked remotely like those on the city vehicles. He dressed up in a police jacket and "patrolled" the streets and highways. When he found a vehicle that interested him, he turned on his red light and attempted to pull the vehicle over. He carried on with this illegal behavior until the day he inadvertently pulled over an off-duty officer. The officer arrested him on the spot, and the pretender is now serving five years in prison.

Similar problems exist in the corporate world. During late 2008 in a visible step at disciplining credential fraud, Broadcom Corporation fired one of its executives for misrepresenting his educational degrees. Senior Vice President Vahid Manian asserted he had earned both undergraduate and graduate degrees from the University of California. A public corporate website at the time confirmed this claim. However, during an investigation from a fraud discovery firm, the school reported that no degree had ever been conferred to Manian. Immediately following the firm's report, he was fired, and the executive's profile on the company's website was removed.[9]

The same investigation firm looked into claims of the educational background by MGM Mirage Chairman and CEO Terry Lanni. Although Lanni had received an honorary MBA from the University of Southern California, some within the company had asserted that the degree was actually obtained through coursework. This contradiction prompted an inquiry. The investigation firm contacted the school and verified that the degree was definitely honorary. Shortly thereafter, Terry Lanni retired from MGM. No direct connection between the release of this information and his retirement has been established, and MGM released a later statement saying that the event had no influence on the retirement decision.[10]

No behavior occurs in a vacuum without some other influence or disposition. As we can see in these examples, individuals are capable of distorting mimicry into a tactic by which to inject an unearned advantage. We cannot know the events, relationships, or other dispositions that would have led to these decisions. However, the consequences are clear. The dysfunctional use of the instinct of mimicry, as a tool of deception for personal gain, produces results that are counterproductive to our social interactions. Whereas, the functional form of the instinct of mimicry intentionally pushes us toward the negotiation of healthy social interactions. Therefore, the easiest way to reveal our disposition for mimicry is to ask the question: Do our choices for mimicry behavior construct healthy social relationships or does it tear them down?

When we look at the function of mimicking in the animal kingdom, the answer to this question is quite clear. Mimicking is made for survival, but not at the cost of the species. Instead, it offers a sustainable method for carrying on life, negotiating social structures, and ensuring continuing strength for generations to come. Likewise in the human realm, we must recognize when we have the potential for being an omega mimic, with all of its deception and dysfunctional activity, and make the choice to reshape our disposition to honor the goal of greater connectedness. Socrates once said, *"The greatest way to live with honor in this world is to be what we pretend to be."* In order to know what we are pretending to be, we must know the behavior we are portraying to others as well as the sources of those behaviors. Questioning and changing our dispositions are only possible in the alpha of mimicry.

The Alpha of Mimicry

How can mimicry help us produce positive and healthy interactions with others? Essentially, how can we become alphas of mimicry? There are really three parts to the answer. The first and foundational way is to admit that we mimic others. This doesn't necessarily mean that we are mimicking those in our immediate presence. Instead, over the course of our lives we are exposed to the many ways that family, friends, leaders, and co-workers react to situations. Naturally, these people, as well as their examples of behavior, have a varying impact on our lives. The observations that make the greatest impressions on us build templates of behavior that we store. Some are stored for a lifetime and others are quickly discarded. The collection of these templates helps shape our disposition for mimicry. When prompted with a situation, we select, interpret, and mimic some variation of a previously learned behavior. We mimic what we learn. For example, a leader who was mentored by an authoritarian might have stored up an entire library of templates for dominating individuals. In milliseconds, he can recognize someone questioning his authority and respond with such immediacy and crafted tenacity that its only source could have been predisposed or innate behavior.

But here is the problem. This despotic leader has no idea why he reacted the way he did. To him, it was a knee-jerk response. Yet, the source of that template came from observations and interpretations that he might have processed twenty years ago. He will never know this unless he is willing to reflect on his own behavior. Though this reflection seems like an overwhelming task, as we can never know our dispositions for every behavior we express, there is great benefit in examining at least the most prominent templates that we store in our minds. As we come to terms with how the greatest influences in our lives shape our behavior, then most of the smaller influences will also fall into place.

For the second part of our answer, we need to evaluate what we find. It takes little more than writing down the names of the most influential (positive and negative) people in our lives to help unveil the templates that we might be using to mimic behavior. As those templates lay bare in front of us, suddenly many things come into focus. We can evaluate the health of those relationships, past and present. We can evaluate whether or not the behavior that we mimic allows us to nurture others. We can see where some dispositions might shape us for productive versus destructive outcomes. A litany of valuable information can be gleaned simply by examining where our greatest influences come from and how we might be replicating the consequential behaviorisms in our own lives.

Lastly, we need to look back at what we know about our mimicry behavior, ask ourselves where it comes from and decide to what extent we should change. As we make efforts to examine the sources of our behavior, something dramatic occurs—our frame of reference changes. No longer are we merely going through life purely responding to what happens. Instead, we are now looking at how we function from a more objective reference point.

We mimic others and that will never change. However, the manner in which we mimic can change as we sculpt our disposition for behavior. Essentially, we are embarking on a new way of thinking about how we act in social environments, and all we have to do is think about it. As Oliver Wendell Holmes once said, *"The mind, once expanded to the dimensions of larger ideas, never returns to its original size."* It is these larger ideas about how we operate in social situations that will shape our future behavior and our ultimate impact on each other.

Think on this story. David was raised on the south side of Chicago. He was routinely beaten up as a young boy walking from place to place in his neighborhood.

One day David scrutinized an older boy walking down his street. When this boy passed a group of kids that had once taunted David, amazingly they backed away and let him pass. All that David could figure out was that a tough-looking walk was all that anyone needed to make it past the bullies in this world. With his new swagger and grimaced expression on his face, David walked the streets with confidence.

At the same time, he started to go to a gym and learned boxing and various martial arts. The boxing coach who mentored him was the epitome of tough— he was an expert street fighter—and as it turns out also a gang leader. David had a natural ability for fighting, and his mentor realized it early on. Despite his mother's prayers to the contrary, David joined his mentor's gang as a teenager and began idolizing everything his mentor did. Over several years he was heavily involved in the gang's activities. And then the fateful day came. During a skirmish of neighborhood gunfire, his mentor was killed. It quickly became clear to everyone that David's talents made him the next in line to fill the role.

One hot summer evening, mere weeks after he took the lead, there was a gun battle at the border between David's and a rival gang. A bullet grazed his head. Wounded and emotionally shaken up, he walked back home to his mother's apartment. In the silence of the night, he could hear her praying for him on the fire escape. With his shirt wrapped around his head to stop the bleeding, he walked up their fire escape and told his mother and sister to start packing. The next morning, they all got on a bus and left the city. It was time to end the madness and start over.

Unfortunately, the baggage of violence stayed with him at their new homestead. In the small town that hardly had traffic offenders, David still walked through the quiet streets with gold chains around his neck and his chest puffed out. He was mimicking the tough persona which had become such a part of his life. His disposition was set. As a result, it became hard to hold down a normal job. People took his toughness as bullying and few would hire his larger than life attitude. Rejection met him at every interview, and he had no idea why.

Every week on his walk from the family's rented house to the downtown unemployment office, he passed by a small white church. One sweltering afternoon the pastor was sitting on the front steps drinking lemonade. Puffing out his chest as he swaggered by the church, David could tell that the pastor was looking at him. "Those gold chains look too heavy to carry around on such a hot day," said the pastor as he offered up a glass of lemonade. Somehow, the pastor's words pierced his heart. David knew what he meant. He had been pretending to be something he wasn't for too long, and it took almost losing his life to realize it. A tear rolled down David's cheek as he sat down, took off his chains, and started talking to the pastor. A dozen difficult years of violence and the emotional torture he inflicted on his family evaporated in the hour he spent at the church that day. His disposition had changed, and he learned how to unify people rather than destroy them. His instinct of mimicry changed course. Within a year of talking to this pastor, David opened the town's first community center in a building adjacent to the church. After five years he began speaking at multicultural centers throughout the Midwest and helped to bring hundreds of gang members out of mental, sociological, and spiritual bondage.

David's story is powerful because it shows the raw underbelly of how we carry our dispositions with us even when it is our intention to leave them behind. In order to let go of the oppression that beseeched him daily, David had to take a step beyond just a change of scenery. He had to redefine the sources of his disposition of mimicry. For David, many of his dispositions for social behavior had to be abandoned. In their place, his faith, a mentoring relationship with the church's pastor, and the unity he found in bringing communities together became the source for the behavior he chose to mimic. From a life of omega mimicry, he became an alpha.

Mimicry in Action

In 2008, Stanford cognitive psychologist Jeremy Bailenson and a team of researchers embarked on a study to determine how well humans can perceive mimicry—in computer-simulated environments.[11] Using virtual reality, the study's participants interfaced with a computer-animated simulation for three minutes. The simulation was made up of a 3-D human face on a computer screen built to realistically convey body movements and emotion to such a degree that it looked like another human was controlling the avatar. What was unknown to the first half of the participants was that the avatar mimicked the participants' head position and movement—but with a four second delay. Every time they moved their head in any of three directions, the avatar stored the movement and then performed the same movement later. The second half of the participants watched the same presentation, but their avatar was pre-recorded and was not mimicking their behavior.

Once all of the participants had finished their sessions, they were asked a series of questions about their experiences. An analysis of these responses showed that only five percent of the participants realized the avatar was mimicking them. Additionally, all of the mimicked participants responded with a deeper emotional connection to the avatar and were more convinced by what it was communicating. The study makes a valid point that as a social function, mimicry is capable of altering our feeling of connectedness with others—mimicry shapes how we are drawn to each other. Even though the complexity of the mimicry was limited in their tests, Bailenson's conclusions point to mimicry being a persuasive power in the social interactions we have.

In this context, the study has unique ramifications for our actions as leaders. Naturally, we influence those that follow us. Most of the time we are intentional about the influence that we want to convey—meaning that we have a strategy behind how we motivate, communicate, direct, and coalesce the people that rely on us. However, we need to ask ourselves what other messages might we be communicating that we don't intend to convey. Could we be showing others how much or little we are engaged in the act of leadership simply by our social behavior? Likewise, are we drawing people to us or destroying social connectedness?

The instinctual display of mimicry is not a choice. At its core, it is a critical competency of who we are. We mimic and pretend as a necessity of social survival. What is our choice is whether or not we take an active role in shaping the disposition of this instinct. When we lead others, are we merely echoing some example of leadership, good or bad, that made its way into our disposition years ago? Are we exhibiting behavior that has been so reinforced over time that we hardly even know it is there? Or do we have an intentional message that shapes every decision and social environment we face?

Despite his brief time in the White House, President John F. Kennedy communicated commanding and empowering messages that few Americans of his era will forget. As the nation's leader, he faced the formidable challenges of civil rights, an aggressive Soviet empire, and the divisiveness of a country. Despite the authoritarian rule of his father, JFK created his own path of leadership, excelling educationally and developing keen political acumen. Rather than mimicking his father's behavior, JFK altered his own disposition for the sake of a new and personal message. He desired to communicate to the entire country his desire for social connectedness and responsibility. As an alpha, his leadership message was about we and not me. In the last section of his inauguration speech, Kennedy said:

> *In the long history of the world, only a few generations have been granted the role of defending freedom in its hour of maximum danger. I do not shrink from this responsibility—I welcome it. I do not believe that any of us would exchange places with any other people or any other generation. The energy, the faith, the devotion which we bring to this endeavor will light our country and all who serve it—and the glow from that fire can truly light the world.*
>
> *And so, my fellow Americans: ask not what your country can do for you—ask what you can do for your country. My fellow citizens of the world: ask not what America will do for you, but what together we can do for the freedom of man.*
>
> *Finally, whether you are citizens of America or citizens of the world, ask of us here the same high standards of strength and sacrifice which we ask of you. With a good conscience our only sure reward, with history the final judge of our deeds, let us go forth to lead the land we love, asking His blessing and His help, but knowing that here on earth God's work must truly be our own.*[12]

Years later, his daughter Caroline echoed this theme in the introduction of a biography about her father. In it she wrote, *"I hope that by learning about this vital episode of American history, children will come to share my father's conviction that each person is able to make a difference, and everyone should try. No one is too young to start thinking about what he or she can do to better America."*[13]

Like President Kennedy, what we become as leaders is best revealed in the mimicry behavior that we (choose to) exhibit. If we blindly carry out the dispositions that are set for us, with no reflection, then there is no context or objective reference from which to make significant change. However, as we take the step to examine how the greatest influences (both people and events) of our lives shape the things we do and say, then we are in a position where healthy and sustainable social connectedness is a reality.

In 1966, Charlie Finn authored a poem about our masks of humanity. Since then it has circled the Internet and has been published in multiple books and songs. It's a wonderful survey of how mimicry and pretending is the basis for much of our human interaction. 🌟

Please Hear What I'm Not Saying

Don't be fooled by me.
Don't be fooled by the face I wear
for I wear a mask, a thousand masks,
masks that I'm afraid to take off,
and none of them is me.

Pretending is an art that's second nature with me,
but don't be fooled,
for God's sake don't be fooled.
I give you the impression that I'm secure,
that all is sunny and unruffled with me, within as well as without, that confidence is my name and coolness my game,
that the water's calm and I'm in command
and that I need no one,
but don't believe me.

My surface may seem smooth but my surface is my mask,
ever-varying and ever-concealing.
Beneath lies no complacence.

Beneath lies confusion, and fear, and aloneness.

But I hide this. I don't want anybody to know it.

I panic at the thought of my weakness exposed.

That's why I frantically create a mask to hide behind,
a nonchalant sophisticated facade,
to help me pretend,
to shield me from the glance that knows.

But such a glance is precisely my salvation, my only hope,
and I know it.

That is, if it's followed by acceptance,
if it's followed by love.

It's the only thing that can liberate me from myself,
from my own self-built prison walls,
from the barriers I so painstakingly erect.

It's the only thing that will assure me
of what I can't assure myself,
that I'm really worth something.

But I don't tell you this. I don't dare to, I'm afraid to.
I'm afraid your glance will not be followed by acceptance,
will not be followed by love.

I'm afraid you'll think less of me,
that you'll laugh, and your laugh would kill me.

I'm afraid that deep-down I'm nothing
and that you will see this and reject me.

So I play my game, my desperate pretending game,
with a facade of assurance without
and a trembling child within.

So begins the glittering but empty parade of masks,
and my life becomes a front.
I idly chatter to you in the suave tones of surface talk.
I tell you everything that's really nothing,
and nothing of what's everything,
of what's crying within me.

So when I'm going through my routine
do not be fooled by what I'm saying.

Please listen carefully and try to hear what I'm not saying,
what I'd like to be able to say,
what for survival I need to say,
but what I can't say.

I don't like hiding.
I don't like playing superficial phony games.

MIMICRY

I want to stop playing them.

I want to be genuine and spontaneous and me
but you've got to help me.

You've got to hold out your hand
even when that's the last thing I seem to want.

Only you can wipe away from my eyes
the blank stare of the breathing dead.

Only you can call me into aliveness.
Each time you're kind, and gentle, and encouraging,
each time you try to understand because you really care, my
heart begins to grow wings--
very small wings,
very feeble wings,
but wings!

With your power to touch me into feeling
you can breathe life into me.
I want you to know that.

I want you to know how important you are to me,
how you can be a creator--an honest-to-God creator--
of the person that is me if you choose to.

You alone can break down the wall behind which I tremble, you
alone can remove my mask,
you alone can release me from my shadow-world of panic,
from my lonely prison,
if you choose to.
Please choose to.

Do not pass me by.

It will not be easy for you.

A long conviction of worthlessness builds strong walls.

The nearer you approach to me
the blinder I may strike back.

It's irrational, but despite what the books say about man often I
am irrational.

I fight against the very thing I cry out for.

But I am told that love is stronger than strong walls
and in this lies my hope.

Please try to beat down those walls
with firm hands but with gentle hands
for a child is very sensitive.

Who am I, you may wonder?

I am someone you know very well.
For I am every man you meet
and I am every woman you meet.

Charles C. Finn
September 1966

Principles for Reflection

- The time we spend examining why we mimic contributes to a grounded sense of our own leadership influences.

- Everyone pretends to a degree, and everyone has mimicked or is mimicking someone else that has a profound influence on his or her lives right now. Who are these people in your own life?

- Mimicry is said to be the highest compliment

someone can give you. Yet, we have to ask our-selves if we are broadcasting behavior that we would not want anyone to copy in us.

• There is healthy mimicry and destructive mim-icry—what can we do to recognize the difference between the two?

• We pretend and mimic, often out of necessity. However, great leaders are willing to abandon anything that they are doing that is detrimental to those they lead. Do we have the clarity to know when this is necessary?

• Oftentimes, we are the ones who are most de-ceived by our own masquerade. We should be willing to lay down the mask and look in the mir-ror with a focused and unclouded vision.

3. COMMUNICATION

"People have to talk about something just to keep their voice boxes in working order, so they'll have good voice boxes in case there's ever anything really meaningful to say."
—*Kurt Vonnegut*

"Electric communication will never be a substitute for the face of someone who with their soul encourages another person to be brave and true."
—*Charles Dickens*

All communities of life forms need to communicate. The willow tree uses pheromones to warn other trees of an insect infestation. A Colorado magpie calls to its mate from the top of a mesa. A humpback whale sings across hundreds of miles of open ocean while a leader shares her strategic vision for the organization she serves. These interactions are hardly limited to exclusively information transmission. We are not merely a horde of mortal radio towers broadcasting our thoughts into the cosmos—and listening to no one. As Jeff Daly once said, *"Two monologues do not make a dialogue."* Instead, we have an innate force driving us toward a specific end. Within our instinctual makeup, we are wired for connectedness. This only happens when we harness an ability to infuse our thoughts into the minds of others while at the same time apprehending their thoughts as well. We communicate consciously and subconsciously, and without this component of our behavior, there could be no such thing as social communities, organizations, or leadership for that matter.

For leaders, the grandness of our leadership ability must cower to the degree to which we have developed an ability to communicate. If we can't communicate, then our talents of motivating and networking people will be fruitless. In John Maxwell's book *Everyone Communicates, Few Connect*, he comments:

> *Connecting is crucial whether you are trying to lead a child or a nation. President Gerald Ford once remarked, "If I went back to college again, I'd concentrate on two areas: learning to write and to speak before an audience. Nothing in life is more important than the ability to communicate effectively." Talent isn't enough. Experience isn't enough. To lead others, you must be able to communicate well, and connecting is key.*[1]

Still, there are abundant ways that we connect with others, not the least of which is speaking and writing. Sometimes the most powerful way that we connect with someone is by communicating silently. Like the long embrace from a chaplain following a memorial service; the firm pat on the shoulder for a job well done after the contract is signed; the executive's office door that is always open; a simple fist pump after a successful mission, and so on. Wordless expressions like these provide as much if not more of a message than anything that could be orated from a platform microphone. And each one of them is representational of the thousands of ways we express a sense and a desire for validating our connectedness to each other.

Like any other instinct, the molding of our disposition for certain communication behavior is sourced from deep within. So, as we look at the instinct of communication, keep in mind our investigation is more about our connectedness to others rather than nuances of how we communicate. We want to become expert craftsmen of our behavior. The only way to do that is to look sincerely at examples that help us reveal what makes us communicate the way we do. In the end, we will realize that we are doing more than just passing and receiving information. Like those in the animal kingdom that have perfected the instinct of communication, we all create the circuits that enable us to understand, preserve, and unite our sense of community.

Beyond Mere Animal Instinct

One summer afternoon, I had the pleasure to meet with chief animal behaviorist Megan Sanders of the Cheyenne Mountain Zoo in Colorado.[2] As we walked through side avenues to the primate house, she laughed and recalled a powerful example of how communication is an important tool across animal species. She recalled an open-front exhibit at the zoo several years earlier that housed a troop of golden lion tamarin monkeys, a few bird species, and several large tortoises. The tamarins at the zoo were known for their ability to alarm whenever they didn't feel something was the way it should be. However, on this one occasion, the alarm sounded different to the zoo workers. Curious as to what was triggering this oddity, Ms. Sanders approached the exhibit—not quite sure what to expect. She looked at the monkeys, the birds, and then looked at the tortoises. The tamarins continued to alarm. Uncertain as to what was going on, she panned the entire enclosure. Everything looked normal until—there it was—a giant tortoise on its back with its legs wavering upward to the sky.

Apparently the tamarins and the tortoises had been neighbors for a long enough time that the monkeys had gotten used to what tortoises do, and sunbathing upside down was not one of those things. Ms. Sanders explained:

> *The alarm was different enough from their regular alarm call that those of us who worked at the zoo regularly started being able to tell the difference between that tortoise-overturned call and other calls that they made. I don't know if I can even articulate what was different about it, but I would guess about 90% of the time when one of us would yell to a co-worker that it sounded like a tortoise might be upside down you would go out and, sure enough, find a tortoise upside down.*

What is most fascinating about this behavior is that the monkeys interpreted the behavior of the tortoises and established when there was an anomaly of that behavior occurring.

Next, the monkeys determined that this anomalous behavior was significant enough to warrant an alarm. What we cannot know is why they communicated the alarm in the first place. What benefit did it provide? Typically monkeys innately use the alarm call to alert the rest of the troop for the existence of danger, like a leopard or a snake. Alternatively, it is used to scare the threat directly. Since the upside down tortoise posed no actual threat, there are a few reasons why the alert might have been needed. First, it might have looked like a foreign creature that represented a potential threat. Second, since the flipped tortoise was a change to their environment, it naturally represented uncertainty.

What they learned, however, is that sounding an alarm caused an effect—tortoise flips upside down, monkeys create audible alarm, humans show up and turn the tortoise over. It is hard to say what is a primed versus a learned disposition in this case, but this example shows us how even the most obscure form of communication, a monkey's alarm call, can be effective enough to produce a proper response, even if the solution came from a different species—a zoo worker.

Obviously, communication in the animal kingdom is much more than just sending out an alarm. Animal behaviorist Alexandra Morton explains in her study of whales, the instinct of communication is about the apprehension of information in all of its forms. Blue whales, for example, are the loudest animals on Earth. She writes:

During the cold war, the U.S. Navy mounted hydrophones on the sea floor worldwide to listen for enemy submarines and ships. Through this array, navy scientists picked up very low frequency 15-hertz rhythmic pulses. These sound waves were 300 feet across. As they tracked these sounds, sometimes for more than 900 miles over forty-three days, they discovered they were listening to migrating blue whales navigate. A blue whale in the North Atlantic can send out a call and fifteen minutes later hear an echo telling him which way to Bermuda.

While most species draw together at mating time, fin whales have the odd habit of spreading out over the vast South Pacific when they get the urge to procreate. In this case it was geologists with an ear cocked for the subsonic rumblings of earthquakes who picked up 20-hertz pulses in a pattern too rhythmic to have been made by mother earth. These turned out to be fin whales 200 miles apart conversing. The whales' summons got a little scrambled at these ranges, with acoustic components arriving at different times, but the whales keep their calls simple and regular and apparently get their message across: "Helllooo. I'm way over here, but I'm worth the trip."[3]

Besides the importance of audible communication, another aspect relates to the role of visual cues. Back at the Cheyenne Mountain Zoo, Megan Sanders had once observed a female gorilla and her newborn that were making their first visit to an outside enclo-sure. It was an uncertain moment for the baby. Despite numerous attempts from the mother to coax her child outside, the baby would not go past the doorway that opened to a large, plush tropical yard. Trainers noticed this went on for weeks; then finally, one day the baby stepped outside.

From that day on, the baby would wait in the doorway of the enclosure long after the other gorillas made their way into the yard sitting and staring at her mother. Then for no apparent reason, the baby would suddenly make a mad dash for her mother sitting in the yard. The trainers were stumped. Why was the baby waiting so long to go into the yard?

The answer came when everyone turned their at-tention to the mother one morning. Each time the troop traversed the entrance to the yard, the moth-er would walk to a far, side wall and sit down. She watched each of the other gorillas move to different places. All the while, the baby sat by the entrance and kept her eye on her mother. Once the mother felt that the troop had settled down enough, she slapped the side of the enclosure wall one time making a loud whump sound. This indicated to the newborn that it was safe to enter, and with lightning speed, the baby ran to her mother's back. To this day, no one at the zoo has determined how this behavior developed or why the mother-daughter pair adopted it.[2]

Even in animals that are not believed to be as cog-nitive as primates, there is similar fascinating communication behavior. Leonard Lee Rue III detailed his experiences researching the deer of North America. He writes:

...when a deer becomes alarmed but cannot identify the object of its suspicion, it stamps a forefoot. It may stand in one spot and repeatedly stamp while doing all it can to discover what alarmed it by using its nose, ears, and eyes. Or the deer may advance cautiously, stamping one forefoot and then the other. The tremors set up by the stamping travel a long way through the ground, alerting all deer in the area. Some of the deer may be feeding or screened by vegetation from the alerted deer, and they cannot see a visual signal...Communication has been achieved through the sense of touch.[4]

In this case, communication is neither audible nor visual, but the tactile sense of a ground tremor is all that is needed to send a warning. In addition to chemical and seismic-tactile communication, African elephants have an ability to use low frequency communication, well below the audible range of humans, which allows them to transmit what are called infrasounds nearly six miles. From their book *Mammalogy*, Terry Vaughan and colleagues assert:

Radio-tracking studies in Zimbabwe showed that families of different clans would suddenly alter their direction of travel when still several miles apart in an apparent attempt to avoid contact. Also in Zimbabwe, [elephant researcher] Garth

Thompson observed a group of 80 elephants suddenly abandon their habitual home area the same day that many elephants were being shot in a culling operation 90 miles away in Hwange National Park. Several days later, Thompson found the 80 displaced elephants bunched together as far away from Hwange as they could get. Some message of danger and death had seemingly been relayed many miles from group to group of elephants. Long-range communication by infrasound adds yet another dimension to the complex social world of elephants.[5]

If we look at the underlying basis for communication in these examples, we can once again see how instincts contribute to survival at the individual and community levels. Animals sustain their communities via communication. They alert and signal each other through communication. Sometimes they navigate using communication. And the social mediums they use are all programmed and developed within the innate regions of their instinct.

From the bright plumage of birds in courtship, the chemicals that the Australian tree frog uses to communicate with other frogs, the scent glands on the male deer's head as he rubs against a tree, to the posture of bottle-nosed dolphins competing for a meal, communication behavior is a significant component to how every species on this planet operates—including humans.

The Human Dimension – Communication

If you were to read an organizational behavior text-book from twenty years ago, it would have described communication as nothing more than a pipeline or a conduit between people for the purposes of transmitting information or meaning. In this mindset, communication appeared to be nothing more than messages passing back and forth as if we were talking over an old Army radio. *"Hello, are you there? OVER."* *"Yes, I am here. OVER."* The intricacy involved in communication, as research provides today, shows that our ability to communicate is much more complex than we often acknowledge. Communicating isn't just about saying something. It is about understanding a story—a narrative—and we use more than verbalized words to make this happen. In his book *You Don't Need A Title To Be A Leader*, Mark Sanborn says: *"Communicating isn't the objective in business or life. The objective is understanding. Communication is simply the tool to do that."*[6] And the reason why the instinct for communication seeks to establish understanding is because the root of our survival ability is found within community.

The Greek origin of the word communication comes from *communis*, which literally means "to make common or to participate in." In the long-term function of any leader-follower relationship, communication is about the establishment of community, collaboration, and understanding. Even the loneliest and most isolated times of our lives are sandwiched between times of deep community connections—whether they are with fellow workers, family, or friends. We are never without a desire for community for very long.

Beyond connectedness, communication is necessary for our survival. During the 1940s and 1950s, several sociological and psychological research studies attempted to divulge the reasons why many sick babies in hospitals and orphanages were dying. It was initially believed infection and other diseases were the primary cause, yet despite the increased use of antibiotics to combat infection, mortality rates of the children in these hospitals and orphanages had not dropped.

Researchers finally discovered the cause, and it was shocking. A majority of the fatalities were not caused by disease or any physical condition the babies appeared to have. Instead, the statistics pointed directly to the amount of attention, communication, and contact that was provided by caretakers. The sicker a child became, the more they were isolated from everyone. The babies were intentionally denied visitors and contact because of a fear that they would spread disease. As a result, most of them died from a lack of contact and communication with others. Further studies by Cambridge psychologist John Bowlby, among others, confirmed a direct association between the contact and affection a baby receives and its ability to survive.[8]

Communicating is not an option. It's as integral to our makeup as any other instinctual system we possess. Our physical and communal survival depends on it, and the people whom we are around, the environment we are in, and the choices that we make shape its personification in our lives. So, as with other instincts, we must become cognizant of how it shapes —and is shaped in—our social lives. When we choose to actively participate in developing our instinct of communication, it reveals itself through our behavior. Alternatively, our lack of interest sets the stage for becoming the epitome of disconnectedness.

The Omega of Communication

Out of the corner of his mouth the CEO said to his CFO, "*I suppose that I could have done that differently.*" Bill had just spent an hour trying to explain why the company was about to embark on a series of layoffs. The all-employee audience sensed his tone and saw him uncomfortably wiggle his right hand as he spoke. He was clearly more nervous than any other time addressing the company. With a knot in his throat he finished his speech:

> *Due to the financial strain of this economy, we have been forced to take measures to ensure our sustainability. Unfortunately, that must include a realignment of resources in several business sectors to allow us to weather this storm. We can't all make it through this together, and I am sad to see many great contributors to our company leave us. However, we have no other option.*

As he sat down, he accidentally kicked the corner of the table and, in an effort to regain his balance, knocked over a glass of water onto his speaker's notes. Over two hundred people witnessed the leader of their organization in awkward distress, and it made them very uneasy. He had conducted layoffs before, but not like this.

Earlier in the year, he signed a contract that began the acquisition of a smaller and highly debt-leveraged company. It was a risky move, but the payoff on taking over the other company's unique product line could have been a sign of strength to its investor base. No one fully understood why the CEO pushed so hard for the buyout at the time, but now the answers were more and more revealed.

First, the board found out that the CEO's nephew was a director in the other company. Next, despite early indications otherwise, the acquisition-company's debt was actually due to bad investments, and not research and development expenses as initially thought. Now, the parent company could no longer afford the impact of the acquisition in a declining market, yet the ink had been signed on the contract.

Through back channels, this information had made its way all the way to the line-level employees. As the CEO wiped up the spilled water with a few napkins, his body language only affirmed the rumors that had been spreading for weeks. The employees standing before him knew that it was his fault that fifty or more people would be soon looking for work and benefits elsewhere. Without him admitting any culpability, everyone in the company knew who was responsible for these layoffs—and it made them irate.

The underlying context for this example was not the failure of corporate strategy, nor did it have to do with a megalomaniac CEO. Instead, the instinctual disposition of one person, the leader of this organization, created the series of events that would lead to this day. And it started long before he ever took this position.

Years ago when he first joined the company as a young manager, Bill had underestimated the budget necessary for his first project. It was a mistake of immaturity. However, it was the catalyst for every other decision he would make in his career. Rather than bring the blunder to the desk of his boss, he devised a plan to cover it up. He hid the financial mismatch by siphoning small amounts of money from his other department projects until the shortfall was met. He then reported at the end of the quarter how successful the project had become, and the accolades started. He became an instant management success story—from all appearances. Surprisingly, the financial failure was never discovered.

Although everything appeared great on the outside, a greater problem had been created. As Bill completed projects and took leaps in the leadership hierarchy, he realized that by manipulating his communication with others in the organization, he could manipulate their behavior and, ultimately, his success. The first taste of the easy way was enough to entice him to continue and to reinforce his behavior. Instead of becoming an alpha of communication, he was slowly becoming an omega—one who would eventually lose everything because of how he had isolated himself from his own company.

Bill's disposition for communication was set decades previous, and it still wielded great power over him. Rather than communication being a tool for establishing connectedness, it was a tool for personal gain. Eventually, his entire instinct of communication collapsed in on itself the day the board asked for his resignation. The subtlety of decades of misrepresentation slowly numbed him to the reality that his disposition for communication had become corrupt.

We all have the potential to be an omega of communication, driven by choices that are counterproductive to healthy and functional communication. The choices we make every day shape our disposition for this instinct. We can make the choice to become leaders who disconnect ourselves from the bonds that are created from healthy communication, or we can tunnel down and seek out the value within the depths of connectedness. If we choose correctly, we can become an alpha of communication.

The Alpha of Communication

For more than fifty years, psychologists, sociologists, and anthropologists have known of the impact that verbal and nonverbal communication have on the way we connect with each other. In 1959, anthropologist Edward T. Hall asserted nonverbal behavior was associated with verbal behavior in our brains but that the two exist in different "registers".[9] Because of this separation, the two are not always in useful alignment. For example, Hall described that although U.S. diplomats had strong linguistic skills in the language of the foreign country they were visiting, their ability to communicate could fail because, to the native community, language was tightly integrated with subtle nonverbal cues. A native of that country could spot a foreign officer even though they couldn't explain why. Since the visitors could not blend in to the cultural nuances required for unabated communication, their conversations always suffered.

Today, many international agencies are fully aware of this issue and have instituted training and protocols to make intercountry communication more palatable and transparent to the foreign receiver. The CIA, for example, has an integrated training program that provides operatives the education necessary to learn to become essentially invisible while in plain sight. Their ability to adjust to their surroundings is a tool of anti-communication—creating a vacuum for all of the external signals that one could perceive as foreign.[10]

In the late 1960s, psychology researcher Dr. Albert Mehrabian provided a little more detail about how people communicate using verbal and nonverbal cues.[11] He produced two studies which were synthesized to establish the 7/38/55 rule. His theory suggests that when there are inconsistent messages regarding emotion or feelings, humans will commonly consider only 7% of the words used, 38% of the tone used, and 55%

of the nonverbal facial expressions and posture used. Essentially, when it comes to resolving an emotional disconnect or conflict, we will rely mostly on what is not said. Although the 7/38/55 rule has been misinterpreted over the years, the most important benefit that Mehrabian's research offers is. We need more than one method of inquiry to understand each other.

Thomas Kolditz tells a story in his book, *In Extremis Leadership: Leading as if Your Life Depended on It*, how functional we can be interpolating the gaps in our verbal and nonverbal communication. We make the best of each situation. Kolditz says:

> *In 2002, West Point top cadet commander Andy Blickhahn graduated as a leadership major and immediately attended follow-on Army schools at Fort Benning, Georgia. He then reported for his first assignment in the Eighty-Second Airborne Division at Fort Bragg, North Carolina—a historically famous division blooded at Normandy, Sicily, Grenada, and usually the first division to place "boots on the ground" of a foreign war zone. He was at Fort Bragg only seventeen days, with much of his household goods still in boxes, when he boarded an aircraft to Iraq.*
>
> *The new officer somehow found his platoon in the maze of Baghdad; it was pitch dark by the time he joined the team he was to help lead. The team's mission was to conduct an attack across a bridge in the war-torn city. By midnight, Blickhahn's platoon had been attacked and was experiencing*

offensive success against organized Iraqi forces. He later wrote how strange it was when the sun came up and he saw the camouflaged faces of his platoon sergeant and his radio operator for the first time, having fought with them all night long. Until that moment, he had only their voices to personalize the relationship.[12]

We have seen that communication is more than just two monologues broadcasting to each other. It is a collaboration of thoughts and ideas with the aim of creating understanding and unifying us for a purpose—without the foreknowledge of a process to get there. It is more than a simple pathway between two or more people. It is a social ocean of instinctual dispositions moving back and forth via verbal and nonverbal cues. The mixing that occurs results in more than just information passing back and forth. It is the inherent dynamic that changes entire organizations. So, as alphas of communication, how do we harness and shape this great dynamic that occurs all around us?

First, we examine ourselves. We ask the question: how do we communicate with others around us today and why? It should come as no surprise that our instinct of communication is predisposed to specific behavior. And no matter whether we communicate by winking, yawning, yelling, saying something poignant or insignificant, or saying anything at all, our predispositions to communication are uniquely ours. Think about it—no one sounds, acts, or looks exactly like you when you are communicating. The reason for this is that we all use certain combinations of communication behavior to make up an inimitable pattern. As alphas we need to know this pattern.

Next, we must understand the role that our communication has on the responses and reactions of others. What we say and do as leaders matters. And since the efforts of the alpha communicator is to contribute to the unification of the connectedness in his or her organization, the efforts we take in developing our disposition of communication is important. Jonathan Charteris-Black comments on this topic in his book *The Communication of Leadership: The Design of Leadership Style*:

> *We look to our leaders to provide answers to the questions that are as yet unresolved in our minds. They are people who are able to give form to the aspirations of followers seeking a better world. Change is always necessary because followers are not fully satisfied either with themselves or with aspects of the world around them—but are unsure as to what changes are necessary to improve the situation. Leaders are change agents who communicate the changes that are necessary and explain why they should be made. They do this by creating symbols that embody value systems and are able to articulate hidden or suppressed yearnings of followers. Leaders therefore communicate the things that followers already half-know. This is why the messages of transformational leaders are rarely unfamiliar or un-*

recognized. Such leaders are able to remove the heavy responsibility of thought and truth seeking by becoming the symbols of their followers' needs, wants, and desires.[13]

The alpha of communication is a scholar of connectedness both at a personal level and at the social level. The alpha understands what has influenced and is influencing his or her disposition for communication with others. Alphas know the inherent complexities of the verbal and nonverbal messages they send to others and how these forces shape relationships. They are highly effective in shaping interactions with others through the knowledge that everyone possesses the same instinctual inclination to be understood and to understand.

Communication in Action

Jennifer, a marketing manager, knocked on the door of her boss's office to quickly hand him a report that showed just how terrible the company was doing in a certain product market. She had ten years in this department and had watched five of her directors come and go. Her latest director was Stan. He walked around the office like a bulldog and had been the lowest performing director of marketing since he joined the company three years ago. On the way to his office, Jennifer socialized the report to a few of her peers for their feedback and edits, just as she always did. She knew better than to walk in with bad news without the backing of others. Known for his consistent agitation,

Stan grabbed the report from her, looked at the bottom line, and yelled at her for twenty minutes, as if she had personally caused market share to drop. Jennifer left his office in tears.

For the next six months, Jennifer used the stairs near her desk rather than take the elevator next to Stan's office. When the product reports arrived each month, she would wait until Stan was at lunch, then drop them in his inbox. She would stagger her lunch hour so that she was gone when he came back. Jennifer did what she could to disconnect from Stan—until the unavoidable happened. Stan left for a two-week vacation and Jennifer had to hand-deliver the monthly product report directly to the executive vice president, Jim.

Once again, the report didn't contain good news. She held off as long as she could before making the journey to the executive wing. As she knocked on Jim's door, the stately room and fine conference furniture unconsciously demanded respect.

"Hello, Jennifer, come in and have a seat," Jim said.

Jennifer felt like someone had lit every nerve ending in her body on fire. *"Here it comes,"* she thought. He took the report gently from her hand and put it aside on his mahogany desk without even a summary review. He slowly clasped his hands and said:

"I have been looking at our personnel files from your department, and it is clear that some chang-

es need to be made. According to your current manager, the entire team is failing to produce."

Jennifer could feel the blood rush to her face. *"There is no doubt,"* she thought, *"I am getting fired."*

"Based on the performance reports coming from Stan," Jim continued, *"a crisis is at hand. However, I had lunch with some of the product team leads earlier today, and I am confident I have isolated the problem."*

Jennifer lowered her head waiting for the inevitable. He looked at her with piercing blue eyes.

"Stan is not on vacation," he paused. *"He is on administrative leave, until we can find a better fit for him in the organization."* He continued, *"No one has seen this department function longer than you have. I have heard some of your bold ideas get suppressed the past few months. Unless you decide to decline my offer, I am promoting you to director of product marketing effective immediately. Stan's office is being relocated as we speak. Take some time this afternoon and hand off your current responsibilities to your peers, and then clear your schedule for meetings with me all next week. I will get you up to speed in no time."* Jennifer was speechless. After myriad thank yous, tears, handshakes, and a brief hug, she left his office and almost floated above the carpeted floor down the hallway thinking, *"Everything is about to change."*

In one situation, Jim, Stan, and Jennifer brought together three entirely different approaches to communication. Like most of what we experience in our communities and organizations, every social interaction is a patchwork collage of instinctual dispositions. Remarkably, we have the capability to find common ground from which to operate. But this is all dependent on how disposed we are to seeking community. Clearly, some historical context created Stan to become a belligerent and domineering manager. Even without having the background knowledge, we can still discern whether Stan's leadership actions were intended to unify this team or not. Clearly, his actions were antithetical to connectedness within the marketing community. In contrast, Jim was a calculated leader whose greatest concern was to keep the organization at a unified and functional level. He wanted connectedness.

The ability to overcome areas of our disposition that work contrary to community building is an important attribute of a leader. Sometimes we must address areas of our disposition which have been deeply connected to our upbringing. Other times, we must evaluate how cultural or generational issues shape the way we communicate with each other. With a communis goal in mind, each step we take along a path of leadership development should bring us closer to achieving better clarity of what messages we send and what we receive, and how to best communicate them.

As retired CIA analyst and author of *Class 11: My Story Inside The CIA's First Post-9/11 Spy Class,* Tom

Waters explained during an interview:

It was an interesting thing to watch from the sidelines as the Agency brought in young folks who did not know how to stovepipe information. Their bosses that were from the Cold War era were used to individual reports that were submitted with no follow up or feedback. Younger generations would socialize a report so that it could be reviewed before it went up the ladder. Their bosses struggled with how to work with this younger and different dynamic. The concept of social media in today's society is necessitating a need for being more involved after the fact via the use of adaptive and autonomous sourced groups. It took a while for leaders of prior generations to learn how to best lead these younger generations. They quickly realized that if you cut socializing individuals off by themselves they were slower and they couldn't harness the team environment as easily. Together, they were a more adaptive force.[10]

Leadership communication is about embracing the adaptive environments from which we can evaluate

a common method of knowing each others' thoughts. Whether we differ in ethnicity, age bracket, or experience, we have a duty to understand how our own ability to communicate shapes the behavior of others around our teams/organizations and as a whole. What we say matters. How we say it matters. The messages we send without words matter, and it behooves us to value the role that ability and ignorance of communication has on the social realms we touch.

The San Francisco Chronicle once quoted a marketing executive of Nintendo who said, *"No one will deny that Sony is a world-class hardware company, and no one will deny that Microsoft is a world-class software company. Nintendo aspires to neither of those things."*[14] The humor and enigma in this statement is that we are left wondering exactly what the company is planning on actually being if it refuses to be world-class in either category. It is often not what we intend to say but how we say it that has the most dramatic impact. If we can grasp nothing else about our instinct of communication, we must adhere to the rule that everything we say and do must be thought through. To do that, we sculpt our communication instinct with intent.

Michelangelo said it best: *"I saw the angel in the marble and carved until I set him free."* The same is true with our instinct for communication. We need to have a clear understanding of what communication should be in our families, teams, and organizations and make efforts to use that communication. The time is now to take hammer and chisel in hand and make communication an intentional and purposeful activity that nurtures and sustains connectedness in the communities we work and live. Purposeful communication requires both thought and action.

Although legend identifies him as the greatest orator of ancient Greece, Demosthenes wasn't always a great speaker. As an orphaned young boy, he was forced to care for himself after his guardians squandered the inheritance left for his care. On his own and suffering from a severe speech impediment, he found creative methods for surviving. As a tribute to his determinism, Demosthenes practiced speaking with pebbles in his mouth. He continued to practice until the day he was able to speak clearly. According to the legend, when he removed the final pebble from his mouth, his impediment was gone. Like Demosthenes, until we can objectively hone our communication behavior, we are less likely to realize the impediments that keep us from being accepted or understood. 🖑

Principles for Reflection

- We communicate out of a necessity to be understood. Sometimes this includes the messages that we have no intention of sending.

- What we say is only a small portion of what we communicate. Even in silence, our nonverbal communication speaks volumes.

- We are primed for certain forms of communication behavior today because of what we have previously learned about communication. The impact of the strongest stimuli will shape us the most. Culture, family, leadership influences, and experiences all sculpt our communication behavior.

• Re-priming our communication instinct requires us to examine the difference between what we think and what we communicate and realign and synchronize the two together.

• Never assume that what we communicate is what is received. We should always seek to be understood as much as we seek to understand.

• Exceptional communication is about establishing exceptional community. We can measure each day by how well we are connected to those who follow us and how well they feel connected to us.

4. CAUSALITY

"The man that sets out to carry a cat by its tail learns something that will always be useful and which will never grow dim or doubtful."
—*Mark Twain*

"Quite often good things have hurtful consequences. There are instances of men who have been ruined by their money or killed by their courage."
—*Aristotle*

Causality is nothing more than the relationship between cause and effect, and its straightforwardness is often the reason we pay so little attention to it as an instinctual function. In reality, causality is one of the primary tools we've developed to help us learn. Whether we are taking our first steps as an infant or leading a multitude of people in a global empire, the mental accomplishment of grasping causality is a constant struggle for everyone. As a result we are often left with the absurd and paradoxical associations between cause and effect that our minds create. Schuyler Huck and Howard Sandler offer a humorous story in their book *Rival Hypotheses: Alternative Interpretations of Data Based Conclusions* about how ridiculous our observations of causality can sometimes be:

After carefully conditioning a flea to jump out of a box on an appropriate auditory signal, the "experimenter" removed the first pair of legs to see what effect this had. Observing that the flea was still able to perform his task, the second pair of legs was removed. Once again noting no difference in performance, the researcher removed the final pair of legs and found that the jumping behavior no longer occurred. Thus, the investigator wrote in his notebook, "When all the legs of a flea have been removed, it will no longer be able to hear."[1]

Although a silly example of incongruity, the point is profound. We might laugh at how the researchers could come to such a ridiculous conclusion, but we make causal errors all of the time. Even though our minds are wired to build causal relationships as a method for our survival, when it comes to determining how to use this instinct perfectly, we are constantly grappling for the truth. We make misassumptions and connect the wrong causes to the wrong effects. With the best intentions, we build entire paradigms of how things work based on inaccurate associations.

In December 2010, Yale University astronomer Pieter van Dokkum posited an argument which sent shockwaves through the scientific community.[2] For decades, astronomers had used the relative ratio of red dwarf stars observed within the Milky Way galaxy to estimate the number of stars within all of the purported galaxies in the known universe. However, van Dokkum's study revealed that the assumption was false and that the extrapolation of Milky Way data doesn't translate elsewhere accurately. As such, his study argued that the number of stars in the universe is nearly ten times what had been previously estimated. A tumultuous dialog resulted in an unresolved debate that continues today within the astronomical community.

We often don't like when our assumptions have to be reevaluated. Our disposition to causality is something we find comfortable, yet its flexibility is absolutely necessary for our function in society and organizations. With the altering of one bit of data, our preconceived associations between cause and effect can be shifted almost dimensionally—and we have to learn to accept this premise.

It takes only a casual understanding of the brain to understand how causality is a foundational instinct of most intelligent animals. We don't think about it very much, but our brains are constantly at work making associations from observations of cause and effect. From them, we extrapolate theories as to why things happen the way that they do.

For example, an infant uses the causality instinct to comprehend the concept of object permanence. The first time she sees a marble disappear under a plastic cup, her causality instinct has no other association to reference. To her, the marble has vanished from existence. When the cup is lifted, the marble reappears into existence. Eventually, she will come to see that the marble was merely hidden from her view and recognize ("re"cognize) in fact, there was an alternative option to her assumption. She will then have modified the disposition of her causality instinct. The next time she observes something disappearing from view, she will project what was previously observed with the marble and the cup into the new situation. She will have experienced a paradigm shifting learning experience that will become a building block to future causal experiences.

Although simple games with marbles and cups may seem rudimentary to us, causality is no less apparent in other areas of our lives. Our minds constantly attempt to construct conclusions from what little evidence might be available. For example, suppose that you walk past the copier room while working very late on a Friday night and startle someone who is feverishly shredding a box full of paper. Based on this person's nervous reaction to your presence, your mind will immediately start running causal scenarios to help you interpret what you observe. Is this person surreptitiously shredding company documents illegally? Are they merely getting rid of old grocery receipts using the company shredder? Or is this a last minute assignment from their manager?

We may never know the true explanation, yet we constantly try to piece together a representational mosaic from shards of information as we work to apprehend the answer. No matter the amount or accuracy of the information we seize, we always attempt to form a conclusion.

Our conclusions, however, might not be so benign. Imagine a distraught boy carrying a dead dog and approaching a military patrol driving down a dirt road in Afghanistan. Instantly, the brain activity of an observing soldier is at a fever pitch examining the boy's demeanor, intent, facial expression, speed at which he approaches, and so on. From a simple visual image with little information, the soldier must deduce whether the child is merely upset due to the loss of a pet or is a belligerent adversary approaching with a concealed IED.

As we will discuss in this chapter, the importance of interpreting causality goes back to the raw functions that exist for our survival. The ability to comprehend cause and effect protects us from threats, helps us secure resources like food, water, and shelter, and it is the conclusion-constructing process we use to solve problems and discover potential tools. From embracing the reality of a hammer that hits your thumb to understanding the complexities of a social network, causality is a critical and innate function to our humanity.

Whether we are aware of it or not, our instinct of causality shapes our behavior based on the associations it creates. Consider the contractor who drove from the outer beltway to downtown Washington DC every day for several years. He sat idly in traffic day after day, month after month. His mind became desensitized to the mundane start–stop–start–stop movement of his car. Most days on the commute he could not even remember the make and model of the car in front of him despite the fact that he drove on its bumper for an hour. There was no reason for his concept of causality to change.

Then one day it happened. A red pickup slammed into his car from behind. There were no injuries, thankfully. However, from that day on, he checked his rearview mirror five times more than he used to. The realm of his understanding of causality changed; in the recesses of his disposition, he had stored a new database entry: I might be hit from behind. Six months later, he accidentally coasted into the bumper of the car in front of him while staring at a red pickup that he saw in his rearview mirror. And from that day on, the person he hit began watching her rearview mirror more, until one day when she ran into the car in front of her—and the process repeated itself again and again.

It might not be surprising to understand that our interpretations of cause and effect play a vital role in how we behave in social situations and how we lead people. What is surprising is how we often don't intentionally contemplate these interpretations. Instead, when something happens, we make an association and then store it as a trigger to be invoked at a later time. We pass through the incident not knowing that our disposition has been modified. The next time a similar stimulus triggers that response, like the red truck in our rearview mirror, we merely react without thinking.

As we look at the causality instinct, let's remember that to be better leaders we must have garnered an understanding of what dispositions are operating outside our thoughtful awareness. When we react to an event, we must realize that we are pulling a causal association out of the recesses of our mind and acting on it. Thus, it is critical to understand what these associations are telling us to do and then decide if we need to re-prime them to some other healthy association.

Beyond Mere Animal Instinct

The instinct of causality is one of the fundamental tools that animals and humans have for learning. It is a tool of association—meaning that it is a behavioral component that links an event to its outcome. Many animal species on the planet possess a common, basic, associative learning mechanism designed to detect and store information about causal relationships.[3] It enables organisms to shape their behavior to an environment in which events are linked.[4]

Simply stated, associative learning is the process by which animals learn about causal relationships between events and behave appropriately as a result.[5] This shouldn't astonish us. Causality is a natural component of how we as humans make associations in our day-to-day lives as well. Researchers Leyre Castro and Edward Wasserman explain in their investigation of human and animal causality:

> *Parallels between Pavlovian conditioning and human causal judgment, research on instrumental conditioning, and recent work on the distinction between observed and intervened effects, all suggest that causal knowledge lies at the root of both human and animal behavior.*[6]

In a study by University of Auckland's Department of Psychology, researchers revealed the possibility that some birds, the New Caledonian crow in this case, might be able to solve physical problems using causal reasoning. Previously, the idea of animals using causal reasoning was downplayed in behavioral research. Those who argued against it asserted that while animals might be able to make associations for cause and effect, they couldn't use that knowledge to solve other problems. The New Zealand study offered the possibility that an alternate idea might be true.

Instead of animals being able to learn from simple stimuli and responses, or operant conditioning, the researchers found that the crow could problem-solve based on what it learned. Using a tool in their beaks, the birds successfully extracted food from a horizontal tube in a specific direction that avoided a trap. From this and several other trap tests, the researchers could ascribe to the observation that the birds' ability to avoid the trap was in fact a process of cognitive causal reasoning.[7]

The significance of this research and other ongoing studies of animal causal awareness is establishing new and ground-breaking understandings of the minds and capabilities of animals. When we look at more cognitive and adaptive animals such as wolves, whales, dolphins, and primates, we must be willing to address the potential for causal understanding. While it might be different than that of humans, it is equally relevant.

Consider this story. As a way to protect their family, a wolf pair constructed a den at the base of a high cliff wall. It seemed the ideal location that was not only safe and secluded but also close to a nearby river and a forest full of sustaining nourishment. Their existence seemed sublime until one day it was threatened by an anomaly of cause and effect when a massive musk ox wandered near the cliff wall, awakening the female wolf who had been resting outside the den. The male and pups had left earlier for a morning hunt and were on their way back home with full stomachs. As the female jumped up growling and rounding the ox that was over ten times her weight, it backed up in a defensive posture. It stomped and snorted in defiance, obstinately backing itself up and unknowingly blockading the den's entrance.

While wolf behavior researchers L. David Mech and Luigi Boitani observed the standoff between the female and the musk ox on Ellesmere Island in Canada's high arctic, their attention quickly diverted to the male wolf and his pups who were now just entering the scene. It was clear that the pups were in danger. If threatened, the den was no longer an acceptable sanctuary. The pups would be no match against the giant pounding hooves of the musk ox if they ran for the den's entrance. No matter how the female tried to manipulate the beast, her adversary would not budge. And the pups were getting closer and closer. While the female retreated, the male watched on with intensity. Suddenly, the reality of what he was doing became apparent to the researchers. He was harnessing causal reasoning to find a way to keep his pups away from the den, going against the normal self-preservation behavior ingrained in the pups. Mech and Boitani describe:

> *The musk ox stood directly in front of the den entrance, while the pups were a hundred meters away from the security of the den. First, [the male wolf] picked up an abandoned arctic hare carcass and delivered it to the pups, capturing their attention for a short period. However, the satiated pups rapidly lost interest and started wandering. [The male then] trotted directly across a stream to a sandy bluff, dug out a [food] cache (at least 8 days old), and delivered it to the pups. The cache held the interest of the pups, and they stayed away from the den. With no wolves nearby, the musk ox relaxed and wandered away from the den entrance.*[8]

One has to wonder if the male wolf modified his causality disposition based on the musk ox dilemma in order to solve the problem. Deducing that it couldn't confront the large animal and make it move from its defensive position in front of the den, the wolf instead sought ways to entice its pups to stay away from the dangerous area. When one attempt at a distraction didn't work, the male utilized another by digging up a pungent food cache. In the end, by keeping the pups away from the area, the musk ox felt less threatened and moved away. Thus, the problem was solved through a contemplative effort of causal reasoning.

When we examine how animals use causality, we have to keep something in context about humanity as well. We are all creatures attempting to resolve our understanding of changing environments based on the senses we have. Like animals, these outer lenses are the only interfaces we have to objective reality. We are all creatures in the midst of making sense of what we observe and experience.

The Human Dimension of Causality

To see the human side of the causality instinct and its role in how we learn, let's examine what happened in Race #5 of the 2007 America's Cup. Two racing rivals, the Swiss Alinghi and Team New Zealand, battled the rough seas off the coast of Valencia, Spain, in the thirty-second running of the classic yacht race. Up until this fifth race, New Zealand showed strength in technique, strategy, and seamanship by edging out a small margin. As the two teams began configuring their boats for the race, the sky became obscured with a heavy sea spray riding high winds from the north. As the boats jockeyed for starting position, Team New Zealand sailed through the starting line immediately following a blast from the starter's horn while the Alinghi struggled to make up lost ground before the race even began.

New Zealand crossed the first marker twelve seconds ahead of the Alinghi, quickly let out their main sail, and hoisted their spinnaker. From their growing lead, it appeared to be New Zealand's race to win. However, their confidence quickly changed to horror when a small tear in a high load area of the spinnaker opened up and split down the length of the sail. The foredeck crew saw the tear, knowing that the spinnaker was unusable, and quickly started hoisting another spinnaker inside the other. This "peel change" is a foundational component of every yacht racing team's training program. Should the spinnaker fail in a race, the team can connect a second spinnaker inside the other, hoist it, and then release the damaged one. Ninety-nine times out of a hundred, the rhythm of crew collaboration keeps a peel change from going bad. However, this would not be the case for New Zealand.

Not only had the first spinnaker ripped, but it essentially tore itself apart. It got caught in the hoist, which kept the second spinnaker from reaching the top of the mast. As the top of the torn spinnaker flapped out of control, the bottom dragged through the water. The boat rapidly slowed, and the Alinghi took the lead. What initially started out as a mounting twelve-second advantage and a sure win for New Zealand turned into a sudden loss as the yacht reached the finish line nineteen seconds after its opponent. As a result, the Swiss Alinghi recovered from their earlier misfortunes and won the regatta.

In response to the upset, Grant Dalton, CEO of the New Zealand Team, said:

We have always emphasized reliability as an essential element of our campaign. Today that small tear in the spinnaker cost us the race. We had a little nick in the spinnaker, which must have been a result of hoisting it. Just as we went to do a standard peel it blew out so that was the first problem. Then we starting hoisting but I don't think we had the tack on so we ended up with no spinnaker. That was a mistake. But we pride ourselves in our crew work. It's always been one of our strengths and we're good at power sailing normally. I'm very, very happy about the fight back. I couldn't fault it. We were about three boat lengths ahead when the spinnaker blew out. By the time we were sorted out they were about six boat lengths in front. We kept at them, taking meter after meter by meter out of their lead. We threw everything we had at them on the run home. The margin at the finish was 19 seconds. It could have been a lot bigger.[9]

Indeed, causality is a tool we use to learn and encompasses both experiential and developmental learning. New Zealand's CEO comment post-press conference was telling, "*It was an important race and not a race that we should have lost by a mistake doing something we've practiced a thousand times.*" When we train, educate, and even practice for the purposes of learning, we modify our disposition for causality. If we practice a sail peel a thousand times, we establish and refine associations about how best to do a sail peel. Yet, if we are unable to include other dynamic information, like the possibility of a small tear in the spinnaker or a stuck hoist, then our primed behavior can react only to what we are disposed to do rather than what is actually happening. Instead of preparing for what should happen, we must constantly strive to prepare for what could happen.

The answers for understanding the causality instinct lies in an examination of what has shaped cause and effect as we understand it. Our goal should be to develop a sensitivity to the subtle options which typically exist outside what we think is true. Are there other possibilities to what might happen in this situation? Are there other considerations we are not taking into account? Are there assumptions about cause and effect that we are taking for granted? As we will see in the omega of causality, we can't always be so sure of ourselves.

The Omega of Causality

We often consider causality to be the relationship between something happening and something resulting. It is a matter of simple consequence occurring every day of our lives, right? We flip a light switch, and the light goes on. A traffic signal turns green, and we drive through the intersection. The boss comes in for a surprise meeting, and we act on our best behavior. Yet, this is about how far we will go with cause and effect. We conjecture that an action at any moment in time has an immediate repercussion. If A happens, then B is the result. Unfortunately, when we adopt this simplistic viewpoint about our world, we miss most of the complex activity of causality, potentially to our own peril.

What really happens in our world is a seemingly infinite mesh of happenings and outcomes, and this web of occurrences isn't only one-dimensional. Instead, these events are related to each other and echo through time where they not only shape the immediate world we experience now, but they are a part of the organized or chaotic experiences that make up our future. Taken further, even our thoughts echo through time.

Like the causes and effects that shape our environment, our thoughts shape long-term behavior. Danish philosopher and theologian Soren Kierkegaard once said, *"Our life always expresses the result of our dominant thoughts."* When we think about anything, we are not only processing and analyzing data, we are setting a precedence of thought. We inaugurate the things that we will think about again and again. With little awareness over time, our dispositions become formed, set, and hardened in a kiln of repetitive thinking and behavior. Eventually, we modify our instinct of causality entirely. This modification not only impacts our own lives, but could have historical implications for our families, organizations, and nations.

Consider the fall season of 1777, near Brandywine Creek, Pennsylvania, when an American officer and his escort were investigating a position to stop British General William Howe's forces as they advanced from the Northern Chesapeake area. A British officer who was patrolling the area, Captain Patrick Ferguson, inventor of the first breech-loading rifle, noticed two figures on horseback riding along the hillside. Rather than shooting first and asking questions later, he yelled out a warning and demanded they immediately surrender. However, upon his warning, the two figures quickly galloped away. Despite his ability to shoot each rider with a rifle that could discharge six balls per minute, Ferguson could not bring himself to shoot an enemy in the back.

What Ferguson did not know was that along with his escort on horseback was General George Washington. Ferguson's decision became a moment of polarity for the future of the United States that no one could have appreciated at the time. General Washington was the most decorated and revered icon of the revolution against the British. If he had been killed, the British aristocracy might have easily taken a new leadership role over what would eventually become America.[10]

When Captain Ferguson later learned that it had been General Washington in his rifle sights on the hill that day, he wrote, *"I could have lodged half a dozen balls in or about him, before he was out of my reach, but it was not pleasant to fire at the back of an unoffending individual, who was acquitting himself very coolly of his duty—so I let him alone."*[11] For Ferguson, his disposition of causality was shaped by a moral code that had been established long before this event ever occurred. Whether the two soldiers on the hill could have been young corporals lost in the woods or a general and his escort capable of determining the outcome of the American Revolution, Ferguson's actions were the same. A retreating soldier is not to be shot in the back. However, the exponential sequence of events that occurred from that point to today shows how a single choice can have radically divergent outcomes. What Ferguson could not have realized was that the fate of an entire country potentially rested on his choice to pull the trigger. For America and its future, Ferguson made an ideal decision. However, for the British, he failed to seize an opportunity that would have most certainly bolstered their inertia and potential victory in the war.

Choices matter because their residue can linger for a very long time. For Ferguson's dilemma, the polarity of that moment was undecipherable, but it was nonetheless a generation-impacting decision. His choice of acting in a honorable way helped shape who won and lost the Revolutionary War. His choice continues to echo through time, and regardless of our decisions, we should expect that everything we think and do has a place in the future of our lives and potentially the lives of people we will never meet.

For the omega leader, this should be a matter of grave concern. As our disconnection with, and the lasting implications of, our behavior separates us farther and farther from a cogent interpretation of cause and effect, we detrimentally change our disposition. We begin to instinctively process information, people, and events in a different way than others do. We begin to distort perceptions of how our thoughts create actions and how those actions might create other outcomes. We embrace darker associations that are paradoxical to our previous modes of thinking. Not only have we modified our instinct of causality, we have desensitized it. What used to be shocking is now normal. What used to be repulsive is now acceptable, and in such a mindset, we no longer maintain a capability to know any of the lasting implications of our choices.

Gavrilo Princip is a name that few will immediately recognize. In 1910, he was a nineteen-year old who grew up under the Habsburg Monarchy, which ruled from Austria-Hungary over many regions of Europe including Bosnia and Serbia. In Bosnia specifically, there was significant opposition against Habsburg rule. Like many of his fellow students who resisted monarchical authority, Princip was beaten and eventually expelled from high school.[12] He left Bosnia for Serbia and attempted to join the army in hopes of making grander steps to fight the monarchy. However, he was rejected for being physically unfit. Irate in his inability to join a resistance movement, he started one of his own. With weapons supplied by a government-sponsored group, Princip and his associates sneaked back over the Bosnian border headed for Sarajevo.

Many knew that the heir to the throne, Archduke Ferdinand, was traveling to the same city. However, unlike a previous visit of the Emperor of Austria, Franz Joseph I, where he was provided a massive security contingent, local officials in Sarajevo had no formal plans to provide protection for the archduke's arrival. Additionally, to make matters worse, the archduke wished to travel in a convertible limousine. With his wife riding at his side, there was only a modicum of security and police available for his meetings with government officials. As the vehicles drove down an avenue, a conspirator hurled a bomb at the archduke's limousine, and it bounced off and exploded.

The bomb injured one of his aides as well as several police that were following in another car. The motorcade continued to city hall where the furious archduke had words with local officials about this lack of protection, and he left abruptly. As his entourage departed city hall and followed a planned route of exiting the city, one of the lead vehicles made a wrong turn. In an attempt to turn around, the archduke's limousine stopped briefly at an intersection. Standing at that intersection near the limousine was Gavrilo Princip. He fired two shots at the archduke. The first struck its target, and the second fatally wounded his wife. Within minutes, both were dead.[13]

What Princip did not know was that his efforts of making himself into an icon of Serbian resistance were about to escalate out of control. As some Serbians marched in the capital city of Belgrade celebrating the assassination, local officials attempted to publicly distance themselves from the contention and ordered the streets cleared and all shops closed. They also issued a wire of their condolences to Austria-Hungary. However, this did little to quell the growing animosity coming from Austria who saw the assassins merely as Serbian nationals under support of their government.

Austrian officials went to German Emperor Wilhelm II, who was outraged at the death of his friend the archduke, and sought military support against Serbia. Wilhelm gave his general support of Austria and then left on vacation believing that the issue hardly meant a war. During this time, French leaders visited with Wilhelm's cousin, Russian Czar Nicholas II, and assured him that should a war begin, Russia would have French support. By the time the French officials returned, Austria-Hungary issued an ultimatum to Serbia to surrender its sovereignty or face military action.

This news shocked all of Europe, and sides were immediately taken. Russia supported the Serbians and received confirmation that France was on their side. Britain, who was enjoying camaraderie with Germany at the time, paused in taking a strong position.[14] However, much of Europe was frustrated with Germany for not squelching the offensive inertia that Austria was building. By the time that Wilhelm announced his intention to avert any war, there was no stopping the next outcome.

Austria-Hungary declared war on Serbia on July 28, 1914. France backed Russia out of fear that a lack of alliance would make them vulnerable to Germany. The Russian czar acquiesced to his war ministers and, rather than issuing strict orders to only fight Austria-Hungary, he approved a full mobilization of the military against German forces as well. In response, Germany began mobilizing its forces and issued an ultimatum to Russia that it must cease any military action against Germany. At the same time, Germany sent an inquiry to France to determine if it still wished to remain neutral.

Meanwhile, the ultimatum with Russia expired, and Germany declared war on Russia. There were also reports of clashes between French and German forces at the border and even into German territories. Knowing that they might have to take the conflict to Paris, Germany contacted Belgium and offered them a compensatory agreement for use of the easy passage through their country to France provided they remained neutral. When Belgium refused the agreement, Germany declared war on France and started forcing its way through Belgium.

Britain, now incensed at the aggression on Belgium, gave an ultimatum to Germany to cease its attacks. It expired, and Britain declared war on Germany. While the European battles raged on, the United States attempted to stay neutral until Germany sank the passenger ship Lusitania in 1915 with over 1200 people on board. The growing concern over Germany's authority at sea using submarine warfare prompted action from President Woodrow Wilson. The U.S. declared war on Germany, and the complex battles that made up World War I continued on until 1918. Within four years it is estimated that more than ten million people lost their lives.

When we rewind this entire sequence of events, it takes us back to what we can know about the primary cause of this colossal war in world history. Without attempting to examine the innumerable what-ifs that could have occurred, we are left to a situation on a street between Gavrilo Princip and Archduke Ferdinand. The causal agent that initiated the multitude of events following World War I can be brought back to a single moment in time. The unfathomable impact of one person's action as a cause for a hoard of cascading effects should give us pause as we evaluate our own life decisions.

Our dispositions for causality always stand the test of time. Although we may not individually change the outcome of a nation or the course of a war, our thoughts and actions will have implications in our future if not the future of generations to come. As the philosopher George Santayana once said, *"Those who cannot remember the past are condemned to repeat it."* While we may or may not have visibility into that futuristic realm, we can take the time to be aware of what we do now and have done in the past. This will show our disposition for behavior. From there, the omega leader has the potential to change their disposition for causal understanding and become more in tune with the objective reality that encompasses us all. Only through this self-reflection can we have the opportunity to avoid the destructive thoughts and actions.

The Alpha of Causality

For the alpha leader, the instinct of causality is related to more than just a sense of good leadership.

It potentially has paradigm-shifting implications. As leaders, we should never walk away overconfidently believing our knowledge, experience, or position of power is at an apex of determining the outcome of events. Instead, how we lead during the most antithetical of circumstances determines our greatness. An exceptional example of the causal alpha is found in the story of Shackleton's expedition to Antarctica.

In 1914, at the same time World War I had begun with the killing of Archduke Ferdinand, Sir Ernest Shackleton and his crew of twenty-seven sailed from the island of South Georgia off the easternmost tip of South America for Antarctica on their boat, Endurance. They had the ambitious goal of making the last great polar journey, crossing the coldest, driest, and windiest continent on Earth. After only three days of sailing, the crew began reporting more and more icebergs in the water. Having not expected ice as far north as was being observed, the outlook on the expedition started to turn more and more worrisome. Six weeks into the journey, within sight of the intended base at Vahsel Bay, a storm of massive proportions brought freezing rain, high winds, and subzero temperatures. When the clouds eventually cleared, the crew logged that the ship was frozen in a sea of ice "like an almond in a chocolate bar." For nearly a month, the ship was pushed as the ice floes followed the prevailing wind and ocean currents.[15]

In what was a brief moment of hope, they saw open water only four hundred yards from their ice-encased position. Shackleton and his crew struggled to free the ship from its death, but as the days grew shorter and temperatures ever colder, they were forced to confront the dreaded conclusion that they were now prisoners of the ice that was slowly moving them farther away from any hope of rescue.

The reality set in that as the weather continued to turn from bad to worse, the likelihood of them spending the winter on the ice, only eighty-five miles from land, was now imminent. By rationing their provisions, in some cases down to one biscuit per day, and doing what could be done to keep their spirits up, they continued to survive both physically and emotionally. Alexander Macklin, the ship's surgeon, recalled the situation and said:

> At this time, Shackleton showed one of his sparks of real greatness. He called us all together and told us simply and calmly, we must winter in the pack; explained its dangers and possibilities, never lost his optimism and set about preparing for winter.[16]

However, the raw and unrelenting control of nature forced them to again change their strategy. Shackleton said in his diary:

> It is hard to write what I feel. To sailor this ship is more than a floating home. Now, straining and groaning, her timbers cracking and her wounds gaping, she is slowly giving up her sentient life at the very outset of her career.

Shortly thereafter the ship could no longer sustain the pressures exerted on it from the ice floe. It was crushed and sank in less than three days. Shackleton wrote again in his log, "*Our home was being shattered under our feet, and we had a sense of loss and incompleteness hard to describe.*"[16]

Loading supplies and salvaged wood from the ship into lifeboats, he and his crew set off across the ice floe on foot. After nearly five hundred days on the ice, they eventually arrived at an island that could marginally sustain them. Knowing that the crew could survive on the seals that inhabited the island, Shackleton took four of his crew, boarded a lifeboat full of supplies, and headed out into a channel of open sea. The only available passage was back to South Georgia Island from which they had departed many months previously. His plan was to sail and row back to their launch port and get help. The captain stated:

[The conclusion was forced upon me that] a boat journey in search of relief was necessary and must not be delayed . . . The nearest port where assistance could certainly be secured was Port Stanley, in the Falkland Islands, 540 miles away, but we could scarcely hope to beat up against the prevailing northwesterly wind in a frail and weakened boat with a small sail area. South Georgia [Island, which] was over 800 miles away, but lay in the area of west winds [which would carry the boat toward the island], must be the objective.[17]

Traversing eight hundred miles of ocean in an

open boat, the small crew reached South Georgia Island two weeks later. They were exhausted and had been without fresh drinking water for several days when they finally reached the coastline. That night a storm crashed their boat against the rocky shore and rendered it completely unusable.

Although it was only twenty-nine miles across the middle of the island to the whaling station they departed from originally, it was the most formidable and unconquered land that could be envisioned. It was covered in snow and peaks that reached upwards of ten thousand feet. As they pursued this new journey to reach the other side of the island, Shackleton knew it was the last and only option to ensure the rescue of his stranded crew hundreds of miles away. Without sleeping, they hiked and climbed tethered to each other for three days through the rugged wintry terrain.

Shackleton and the team were unrecognizable to the sailors at the whaling station who assumed that the Endurance had been lost at sea when it departed the island two years earlier. Over the next three months, the battered captain made three failed attempts using different borrowed ships from the station to rescue his crew. Finally, with the help of the Chilean government, a steamship was acquired for the fourth attempt. Within five days the ship reached the crew and rescued them.

During the two years of Shackleton's role as captain of this crew, he endured more challenges to maintaining a sense of strategic leadership than most leaders experience in a lifetime. Each choice and response he and his crew made were entirely dependent on adapting toward the challenging and often life-threatening causes and effects they experienced. For Shackleton, his instinct of causality was underpinned by a disposition that shaped every leadership decision he made. He made this comment following the rescue of his crew. He said, *"Difficulties are just things to overcome, after all."*

As leaders, every circumstance offers us a new opportunity to learn. But since we do not learn from a clean slate, we must ask ourselves what disposition we are bringing into the situation from which we are about to make a decision. By reflecting on this disposition before we ever face a choice or determine a leadership direction, we will find the clarity to know why we react the way we do. This is the path to becoming a great and influential alpha leader like Ernest Shackleton.

Causality in Action

In the world of innovative and powerful technology companies in business today, the standard has been set by the Apple Corporation. At the height of the dotcom bubble, Apple was trading roughly around $35 per share, and at the start of 2011, the stock price is ten times greater. The rise to stardom started when the passionate Steve Jobs returned to Apple in 1996 and established a new leadership paradigm for the company. With an outlook based on focused determinism, Jobs reshaped the underdog company by creating products and features that customers didn't even know they wanted. He redefined market strategies such that the company's ideas were the driving force for action rather than the market driving Apple's product initiatives. Apple wanted to become the cause of every positive consumer effect. Jobs's disposition for causality was not based on the evaluation about what might happen. Instead, he set out to create what would happen. In a 2008 Fortune magazine interview, he said:

> *Apple is a $30 billion company yet we've got less than 30 major products. I don't know if that has ever been done before. Certainly the great consumer electronics companies of the past had thousands of products. We tend to focus much more. People think that focus means saying yes to the thing you've got to focus on. But that's not what it means at all. It means saying no to the hundred other good ideas that are there. You have to pick carefully. I'm actually as proud of many of the things we haven't done as the things we [have] done.*[18]

What we can glean from Jobs's persistence and innovative approach to leadership is that causality is a learning function as well as an action function. As we make associations about how things appear to work in our environment, we take steps not only to respond to what we see and have seen (learning) but also to attempt to determine what will be seen (action). When we do this, we form a whole new learning pattern. We are learning about the present and helping to create the future at the same time. We establish how others will model our behavior and what effects are created elsewhere in others from our actions. This is the contribution of causality to leadership—learning with action. According to Jobs, "*Innovation distinguishes between a leader and a follower,*" and, "*Sometimes when you innovate, you make mistakes. It is best to admit them quickly, and get on with improving your other innovations.*" In these quotes, Jobs describes the disposition around which he functions. He understands causality is a relationship of learning and doing. Each one feeds off the other. Learning corrects our actions, and actions help us refine our learning.

There is no difference between the foundational ways that causality functions in Apple Corporation than it does in the animal kingdom. Like a New Caledonian crow or a wolf pack in Canada, we all use our impressions of cause and effect as a means by which to shape our intentional and reactive behavior in our own environments. We use them to estimate how to do something we have never attempted. We use them to relearn how to do things we have done wrong. And we use them to affirm behavior that we have done right. Causality is the instinctual source behind how we interpret and act on our observations. Our choices always have historical implications whether we lead a family, a small company, an Antarctic expedition, or a multinational organization. The question we have to ask ourselves is: What deep-seated disposition is shaping how we create that history? And is it the history that we want to create? Or is it a history that is continually created without our slightest awareness?

Henry V is endeared as one of the most prominent military aristocrats of early England. Through a study of his family heritage, ascension to the throne in 1413, military campaigns, domestic and foreign policies, and outside critiques and endorsements of his reign, one can see the available information of his life like a story that unfolded through time—not wanting to jump ahead. With each phase, cause and effect is apparent. The associations of his rise to power were unambiguous and seemingly ordained. During the later years in his timeline, one might expect his regal demise to manifest in some great battle, his horse taken down, and forced to fight hand to hand until his archenemy robbed his final breaths with the fatal thrust of a sword.

To many, the finality of the cause and effect of Henry V must end in tragedy, triumph, and valor. However, we can learn much from this story. Humanity and history are not in perfect alignment with any ideal we wish to embrace. Sometimes the most ghastly of outcomes befall our objectification of great leadership. In 1422, at the age of thirty-five, Henry V died suddenly of dysentery. That was it. Nothing more. The inertia that was unifying England stopped in a moment. By getting to know Henry V, we can discover dimensions to causality for which we are entrusted to shape ourselves and still others that shape us, ultimately. We have a duty to delve in to the secrets of both. Ɏ

Principles for Reflection

- We harness the instinct of causality in the greatest and smallest things we do in life.

- Stimuli and responses are around us all of the time, and yet we fail to recognize that they are the powerful forces for which we build accurate and faulty assumptions.

- We can modify our instinct of causality by examining how it operates in our leadership role. Do we have a clear understanding of what is happening all around us and the impact that our disposition for causality has on those that we lead?

- We examine crisis through pre-primed concepts of cause and effect. How can these concepts limit our ability to adapt?

- What stimuli shape our conditioned behavior day to day to which we are numb? How can we identify and change our responses?

- Every day of our lives should be a chance for re-evaluating how we see the causality we create and the causality we receive from others. Whatever is getting past our cognitive mind is going straight to our instinct—and from there our behavior will originate.

5. RATIONALITY

"A mind stretched by a new idea never returns to its original dimension."
   —*Oliver Wendell Holmes, Jr.*

"No sooner does man discover intelligence than he tries to involve it in his own stupidity."
   —*Jacques Yves Cousteau*

In the 1980s, Diana Reiss was in France working on her PhD in animal communication when she accidentally discovered a cognitive ability for dolphins to rationalize observed behavior in other species—mainly humans. During a training exercise, Reiss tossed portions of fish to a female dolphin at her eighty-foot tank in the French Pyrenees. If the dolphin swam away after eating the fish, then Reiss backed up about ten feet from the feeding platform and waited, motionless. It was a form of a time-out for the dolphin, or discipline for doing something that shouldn't have been done. Despite the frustration observed in the dolphin, Reiss's use of operant conditioning taught the mammal to stay in place while being fed. However, that didn't keep the dolphin from scrutinizing the food being tossed its way. The dolphin refused to eat fish that had spiny fins. Realizing this requirement, Reiss went to work cutting the fins off all the fish in her bucket.

During the next phase of training, one small mistake altered the course of her research and caused her to immediately dedicate her life to the preservation of intelligent marine mammals. Despite her efforts to cut the fins off all the fish in her bucket, she accidentally tossed the dolphin a fish with its fins still on. Instantly, the dolphin stopped what it was doing. This puzzled Reiss. What was the dolphin doing? Surprisingly, it backed away ten feet from the platform while keeping her eye on Reiss, and it floated motionless on the water. The dolphin was giving her trainer a time-out for doing something she shouldn't have done.[1]

In previous chapters, we have covered the role instincts play in our survival, social interactions, sense of community, and leadership strategy. At this point in our journey, we now need to step into the realm of what shapes our thoughts—our ability to reason and generate conclusions. As we venture into an examination of the rationality instinct, we cannot escape that we are now moving into area reserved for only the most intelligent creatures on Earth. Some argue rationality is uniquely a human quality. However, when we look at the behavior of advanced species, as well as complexities of their brain structure, it is not a stretch to conclude that we are not alone in having rational perceptions of the world around us. Even though we may not fully understand how each other function, animals and humans create their own world views. If we look at rationality through this lens, as an instigator of behavior, we can see its effects in many areas of humans and animals alike. Louis Herman writes in his article "Intelligence and Rational Behaviour in the Bottle-nosed Dolphin:"

> *Rational behaviour is, then, necessarily built on the requisite bedrock of general and specific intellectual capacity. To understand what I mean by rational behaviour, I begin with the following premise: a function of a mind is to create a model of the world. This model then influences our perceptions and our behaviours, and may allow us to function effectively in that world, provided our model reasonably reflects reality.*
>
> *However, there is not just one world, but many worlds within our life experiences. For the human, the model of the world may differ with context, situation, or culture; as a simple example, consider the different world models of a teenager for home, work, school, sports, and peer group relationships.*
>
> *A model that yields effective behaviour in one situation may be inappropriate or even counterproductive in another. When we bring the dolphin from the wild into the laboratory situation, it enters a radically different world. The ability of the dolphin to function effectively, even creatively, within that new world is contingent on its learning how that world is structured, how it operates, who the actors are, what features are significant, what rules and contingencies apply, and much more; effective functioning, in turn,*

provides inferential evidence that the dolphin has created an accurate model of that world.

A rational animal may then be defined as one that can perceive how the current world it occupies is structured and how it functions, and can then make logical inferences and draw conclusions that enable it to function effectively and productively in that world. Further, a rational animal is able to incorporate new evidence into new perspectives of the world and can then modify its behaviours appropriately—in effect creating a new or revised model of the particular world in which it is immersed.[2]

The appearance of rational behavior is not limited to dolphins, of course. When we look at some apes, the same functional ability to reason is also possible. In 1978, researchers David Premack and Guy Woodruff were able to successfully observe rational problem-solving ability within a female chimpanzee named Sarah. The researchers showed Sarah videotapes of human actors trying to solve problems. They wanted to see if the chimpanzee could understand the problem the actor was trying to solve. In one example, they showed her footage of an actor jumping up and down in an effort to reach bananas that were suspended from the ceiling. After seeing the actor fail to reach the bananas over and over, Sarah was given pictures that showed various ways to solve the problem. One of them was a picture of boxes stacked on top of each other. She chose that picture. Each time she was presented with new videos and various possible ways to solve the problem, Sarah always picked the most viable solution. From this research, Premack and Woodruff contended that this behavior demonstrated the ability for chimpanzees to reason—or as they called it the principle of theory of mind.[3]

These kinds of studies in the area of cognitive animal psychology are stretching our current understanding of animal behavior. Though the research conclusions bring about as much enthusiasm as they do resistance from different spectrums of the psychological community, we at least must recognize that the ability to reason is not exclusively a human trait. And as we learn more of the instinct of rationality in animal behavior, we will likewise learn more about ourselves.

The Human Dimension of Rationality

We all use rationality, as it is inherent to our makeup. This doesn't mean that we always use it as we should. In his book *How We Know What Isn't So: The Fallibility of Human Reason in Everyday Life*, Thomas Gilovich states:

> *...many questionable and erroneous beliefs have purely cognitive origins, and can be traced to imperfections in our capacities to process information and draw conclusions. We hold many dubious beliefs, in other words, not because they satisfy some important psychological need, but because they seem to be the most sensible conclusions consistent with the available evidence.*

People hold such beliefs because they seem, in the words of Robert Merton, to be the "irresistible products of their own experience." They are the products, not of irrationality, but of flawed rationality...

Many of these imperfections in our cognitive and inferential tools might never surface under ideal conditions (just as many perceptual illusions are confined to impoverished settings). But the world does not play fair. Instead of providing us with clear information that would enable us to "know" better, it presents us with messy data that are random, incomplete, unrepresentative, ambiguous, inconsistent, unpalatable, or second-hand. It is often our flawed attempts to cope with precisely these difficulties that lay bare our inferential shortcomings and produce the facts we know that just ain't so.[5]

Our challenge is that we all have the opportunity to be guided by how we have mislabeled flawed rationality for good rationality. This happens mostly when we are unaware of how our own minds function.

The Omega of Rationality

With little contemplation, we assume that what is right in our minds must be right generally. Until we meet a sufficiently insurmountable obstacle from outside our own rationality, we continue on a path of self-revelation. Then for reasons unknown to us, we fail. David Landreth Dotlich and Peter Cairo, in their research on why CEOs fail, say:

...Leaders fail because of who they are and how they act in certain situations. Especially under stress, they respond with a pattern of behavior that can sabotage their jobs and careers. They rely on a specific way of thinking, speaking, and acting that ultimately causes them to fail. Many times, they're not even aware that their behaviors have become reflexive.[6]

With little contemplation we look at our own inferences and process them as facts without ever evaluating an alternative that is outside our mode of thinking. As the Greek philosopher Demosthenes once said, *"Nothing is easier than self-deception. For what each man wishes, that he also wishes to be true."*

One recent example of the power of omega rationality is the ousting of Robert Nardelli, former CEO of Home Depot. As an operations executive for General Electric, Nardelli made a name for himself as a hard-working individual who garnered the nickname of Little Jack in the shadow of CEO Jack Welch. However, his celebrity status within the company was no match for Welch's preference when it came time to look for a successor. In a turn of events that left Nardelli an outcast of GE, he was quickly selected as Home Depot's chief executive. Unfortunately, the corporate culture of Home Depot was less than an ideal match for the strong-willed, command-and-control stance of Nardelli.

Within six years, he had instituted an authoritarian initiative driving store employees to fear for their jobs. He could view every camera from every store in America from his desk. While being paid a salary of more than $200 million per year, the company's stock price continued to fall. In Tim Irwin's book, *Derailed: Five Lessons Learned from Catastrophic Failures of Leadership*, he comments:

> *The sum total of Nardelli's leadership at Home Depot was a dramatic shift in the spirit of the company and subsequently the service of their ever-satisfied customers. The 98 percent turnover in the company's top executives—with 56 percent of the new hires coming in from outside the company—supports this notion. People simply couldn't and wouldn't work passionately for their command-and-control leader. In this respect, Nardelli was no leader at all. He was a dictator who demanded compliance.*[7]

Like everyone, leaders are products of a great stew of chemistry and circumstance. What distinguishes the leader from everyone else is that he or she takes all of that and creates a new, unique self.[8] For Nardelli, the stew was pre-mixed with its ingredients at the time he joined Home Depot. He had a disposition which determined the kind of CEO he could be as well as motivations for behavior no one understood until years after he took the CEO position.

As time passed, many believed that Nardelli was out to show Welch that he made the wrong decision in choosing Jeffrey Immelt as his successor at GE.[9] Could the damage of Welch's rejection have driven his dictatorial stance at Home Depot? As he disconnected further and further from employees, board members, and shareholders, he could not sense the isolation being created in every part of the company. Nonetheless, at the core of his disposition of rationality, Nardelli had created a world view that guided every decision he made over the company. Whether or not this world view represented the reality that everyone else in Home Depot experienced can only be estimated. Thankfully, such omega rationality can be avoided.

The Alpha of Rationality

In their article, "The Quantum Skills Model in Management: A New Paradigm to Enhance Effective Leadership," Charlotte Shelton and John Darling argue that leaders often see the world as they have always seen it and make "their decisions within a relatively narrow band of possibilities, not because opportunities are limited, but because perceptions are."[10]

The perceptions we adopt create a world view, which is nothing more than a map from which we navigate the real world. We would never think of driving through New York City using a GPS device that can only detail the city of Los Angeles. Likewise we should never attempt to navigate the complexities of human behavior within the leadership realm without a firm grasp on our perceptions. We routinely confuse the role of perceptions with a locked-in concept of rationality that adheres to two realms of thinking: inside the box or outside the box. With little comprehension or explanation of what the box is, we arbitrarily define boundaries for the way we think about people, situations, tactics, strategies, and so on. We all talk about a box, yet it is actually shaped and sized differently in everyone's mind. In their book *Connecting Leadership to the Brain*, Michael Haley Dickmann and Nancy Stanford-Blair assert:

> *Perhaps altering the expression "think outside the box" to "think about the box and adjust it accordingly" is more appropriate. The box is fundamental to human nature, because there always have been and always will be mental patterns, or established order, by which the world is understood. There is no option but to create and modify patterns in relation to surrounding influences. Humans have the capacity, however, to reflect on the nature of a particular mental model and to actively structure and restructure it as new information and circumstances inform and reform. Since brain architecture has been handed down over generations and was designed for the exigencies of the prehistoric era, it is, in fact, imperative that a continuous reshaping of the box occurs to adapt to an ever-changing world. It is what the brain does—and does so well.*[11]

The adjustment of that box is the hardest part of leadership because it might include adjusting the corner we have refused to be willing to move. It is potentially a humbling experience. Yet, the benefits are vastly rewarding. Consider the following three questions that we might ask ourselves before every staff or leadership gathering:

(1) What perceptions am I holding on to that obstruct this team/organization's ability to articulate about a new axis of thinking?

(2) If everyone thought what I think, how would this organization run differently (good and bad)?

(3) What am I infusing into the people that follow me and what are they doing with it?

These questions are disposition changers. A habit of practicing reflection can bring us to a new awareness of the perceptions we embrace and how they impact those who rely on us for leadership.

From scientific research agencies, political environments, military leadership, to parallel cultures, successful leaders need to rationally examine their world view. For example, in Native American communities, the generational clashes between tradition, culture, and mainstream ideologies naturally create challenges for tribal leaders. Within each tribe, there is a clan system that is often based on a matriarchal or patriarchal hierarchy. Many elders see that the only sustainable plan for their people is for younger generations to go outside their communities and become educated at the university level. They know that having doctors, lawyers, technicians, and other professionals in the tribe will provide critical skills necessary for their survival.

However, as youths graduate and go to college, they also bring back modern ideologies in addition to their craft or skill set. No longer is tradition of their ancestors the only world view option within the tribe. No longer are the elders the only people who have knowledge, as was in the past. As a result, youths confuse knowledge for wisdom and begin to contradict, usurp, and question the authority of their elders. According to Scott Davis of the North Dakota Indian Affairs Commission, different generations struggle to manage this contention differently.[12]

For example, Native American Generation Xers might be college-educated individuals that are close enough in age to their parents who grew up in the 1940s and 1950s that their concept of rationality is bound tightly around not only the modern world, but also the traditional ways of their tribe. On the other hand, those from Generation Y and the more current generations have the greatest challenges, since their perspectives on education, tradition, and the tribe are fundamentally different.

In order to establish lasting respect for leadership, many clans are now looking to ways of connecting youth back to their traditions while at the same time bringing those traditions into a modern context. This reconnection is accomplished by creating societies within the tribe around some centralized theme. To keep some native youths outside of gang involvement, elders often create a warrior society that is structured around a modern, non-violent context.

For tribe members that focus on traditional skills of gathering food, cooking and feeding the community, and nurturing the family environment, a sustainer society would be created. Additionally, perhaps the unique healing abilities of the medicine men, and their knowledge of natural cures and remedies, would necessitate the creation of a medicine society, and so on. These societies not only keep more youths out of trouble in a growing environment of alcohol abuse, gang activity, and domestic issues, but they also establish leaders within the tribe who are fully connected to the rationality of their modern beliefs and yet fully embrace their traditional heritage.

Essentially, the struggle of many Native American societies is the examination of a box that has suited them well for generations, yet is being pressed and pulled from all sides via contemporary world views. As Mr. Davis concluded:

> *The great war chief and holy man, Sitting Bull, survived because he was willing to break tribal rules and protocols knowing that his tribe's survival was depending on a leader knowing the context by which to best function. At the same time he accomplished this role without losing the traditional Indian context within which he was a leader.*

Whether a Native American culture, a Special Forces platoon, or a corporate department, leaders avoid clashes of rationality by being willing to take new approaches to thinking and doing what needs to be done for their organizations.

In their book *Leaders: Strategies for Taking Charge,* Warren Bennis and Burt Nanus write:

> *Leaders articulate and define what has previously remained implicit or unsaid; then they invent images, metaphors, and models that provide a focus for new attention. By so doing, they consolidate or challenge prevailing wisdom. In short, an essential factor in leadership is the capacity to influence and organize meaning for the members of the organization.*[13]

Our disposition for rationality is complex, and the components that have shaped it over time are equally as complex. When studying how our instinct of rationality operates, we need to look beyond the methods that we use to problem solve or build conclusions. Instead, we must look at the architecture that makes us able to look at ourselves and interpret our world. The goal is not to pessimistically tear down the areas of our life that we don't understand, but rather we must reconcile our interpretations of reality with reality. To do that, we have to apprehend clarity in both.

Rationality in Action

Suppose you took over a manufacturing company which was near bankruptcy. In the midst of your attempt to recover not only financial strength but employee morale, you are hit with the realization that a trucker's strike was about to halt all incoming ship-ments of steel to your factory. This could end any mo-mentum you had gained since first taking over the se-nior leader. Regardless of union talks at the time, you knew that the company could not survive any lengthy shortage of materials. What would you do? How ea-ger would you be to contract with another trucking company, knowing that there was a probable risk of violence to the truckers delivering the critical goods? Even if you went forward with an alternative carrier, how could you rationally risk the safety of these driv-ers knowing that there were rumors of snipers willing to shoot at suspected trucks?

There are several options, but imagine how the best option could emerge from school busses and nuns. In this very real story, the solution came from a creative and radical departure from traditional rationality. For CEO Jack Stack of Springfield Remanufacturing Cor-poration, asking his employees if they had any ideas to get steel delivered to the plant while minimizing risk solved the problem. One person suggested delivering the steel in school buses. Another said to put nuns' habits on the drivers' heads. Stack took both ideas se-riously and acted on both of them. Not only was the steel delivered without incident, but also the truckers arrived in safety from violence and even from the pos-sibility of snipers.[14]

Last, we should ponder what the pre-Socratic philosopher Hericlitus once said:

The soul is dyed the color of its thoughts. Think only on those things that are in line with your principles and can bear the light of day. The content of your character is your choice. Day by day, what you do is who you become.

Principles for Reflection

• What are the factors that prime you to think and act in the ways you do?

• No human comprehends anything perfectly, but we are all responsible for seeking to achieve that level of comprehension. Anything less and we have immediately concluded that our assumptions are sufficient.

• Leadership is a rational endeavor. When it seems to be something else, then it isn't a failure of the principle but its personification.

• We have every opportunity to modify our instinct of rationality through education, but the greatest change occurs when we merely seek and embrace objective truth.

• We shape our rationality daily by choosing the influences to which we expose our minds

• For the leader, the instinct of rationality is critical to make sense of the organization. It doesn't take an oracle. It takes someone who knows exactly what questions to ask and how to move in a direction that continually promotes inquiry.

6. DUTY

"He that takes truth for his guide, and duty for his end, may safely trust to God's providence to lead him aright."
—Blaise Pascal

"The reward of one's duty is the power to fulfill another."
—Jacques Yves Cousteau

Nearly everyone is influenced by a sense of duty. We use it to establish deep bonds within relationships. It is a driving force behind legal systems, faith-based communities, and philanthropic initiatives. Our military, police forces, intelligence communities, and fire and rescue teams all base their reasons for existence on it. We become naturalized citizens, enter into civil contracts, and get married under its auspices. Duty is all around us, and yet we take very little time to investigate its importance in the way we live and the way we lead people.

Duty is not some esoteric sense of responsibility. It is much more enigmatic and complex. Sometimes it comes through sacrifice. Other times it means acting on behalf of another. Duty can be thrust upon us, chosen by us, or repudiated by us. For leaders, it is one of the most powerful and yet neglected tools we have to infuse others with a sense of purpose.

We can see duty as an innate function through its ability to supersede other more rudimentary instincts. Deep down, duty is pure instinct, insofar as instinct overrides risk to the individual.[1] It has the potential to alter paradigms from which all other instinctual behavior functions, including looking out for ourselves.

Consider this example. The duty I have to obey the law is not the same as a police officer's duty to enforce the law. The police officer has made an oath. And in so doing he or she has ascribed a value to the law to where enforcing it might mean their own sacrifice. As a citizen, no such oath exists.

The innate function of duty is also a major component of relationships. From the unique roles we take in family dynamics to leadership positions where we have direct impact on the lives of individuals in our organizations, we construct bonds of trust and distrust by the way we use duty.

As we build deeper relationships, we invoke greater and greater allegiance and loyalty to each other. As we fail in relationships, the ability to rely upon duty quakes. When we have a well-understood and developed disposition for duty, we come to see relationships are no longer defined solely by an affinity or rapport for one another but rather a sense of taking responsibility and obliging ourselves to each other. The strength of our social environment is determined by the extent to which duty bonds us together.

If we look at where we get the word duty, it is easy to see the main difference between its definition and that of the word responsibility. Duty has its roots in the Old French word *deu* which means "due or owed." Contrast that to the word responsibility that comes from the medieval Latin word *respondere*, meaning "to respond." Though we might respond to each others' needs from a sense of responsibility, duty calls us to an obligation to one another—a social contract between us and someone else.

All one needs to do is look at the mottos of the armed services or local police agencies to see the critical role that duty plays in their raison d'être. The U.S. Marines are "Semper Fidelis" (Always Faithful), the U.S. Army Chaplain Corps asserts "Pro Deo Et Patria" (for God and Country), West Point has the motto of "Duty, Honor, Country," and the Los Angeles Police Department has the motto "To Serve and Protect." However, you don't have to know their mottos to comprehend the role of duty within these organizations. Just look at the vernacular they use.

Police officers go on duty and off duty. Soldiers of the armed forces can be active duty or inactive duty. Whether they are engaged in combat or on leave, whether they are rescuing comrades in harm's way or they are taking a needed respite, their entire concept of identity is defined in relation to their duty to the organization, community, or country. Duty binds them to the greater cause, and their sacrifices are always referenced in the line of duty.

Uniformed police and military are not the only organizations that have a sense of duty, however. Universities, faith-based and missionary organizations, nonprofit philanthropic institutions, community service agencies, and even the Humane Society all have established duties to benefit others.

Yet, we often confuse the duty of the organization with the duty of the individual. It is easy to put a plaque on the wall of a building and define the organization's sense of obligation to its mission. Where things seem to get hazy is when we look at how duty affects our own relationships and leadership. As we explore duty, from the raw form of it in nature to the depths of human instinct, let's keep this context: duty determines the bond we have with another and inherently motivates our decision making in those relationships. This is not a discussion about what others dictate for us to do—what we owe them. It is an investigation of our capacity to express a sense of duty to anyone at all—of our own volition.

Beyond Mere Animal Instinct

As we step aside from the other instincts of behavior into that of duty, we enter a realm beyond most classical animal behavior research. Much of what we as humans use to measure duty was birthed out of the German philosopher Immanuel Kant who contended that an act of duty is done only within a respect for moral law. Specifically, Kant said:

A man must first appreciate the importance of what we call duty, the authority of the moral law, and the immediate dignity which the following of

*it gives to the person in his own eyes, in order to
feel that satisfaction in the consciousness of his
conformity to it and the bitter remorse that ac-
companies the consciousness of its transgression.²*

Essentially, in order for us to have a sense of duty,
we must know what moral law is. Since it was argued
that animals do not have a sense or knowledge of moral law, this simple assertion seemed to block any valid
explanation as to how animals could have a sense of
duty.

However, this isn't the end of the story. As later
philosophers synthesized Kant's assertions within the
spectrum of modern philosophy, some realized that
some other approaches to the concept of duty arrive
at different conclusions. For example, University of
Reading professor and expert on modern philosophy
John Cottingham proposed:

*An action done from duty has its moral worth,
not in the purpose to be attained by it, but in the
maxim in accordance with which it is decided
upon; it depends therefore, not on the realization
of the object of the action, but solely on the principle of volition in accordance with which, irre-
spective of all objects of the faculty of desire, the
action has been performed.³*

Although Cottingham makes no explicit statement about animals and duty, using his logic, what
duty we decide to perform might have moral value
without having to adhere to the knowledge of some

higher law. Our decisions and actions can be entirely based on a premise that lies elsewhere. The implications of our choices can have local significance rather than a significance to some grander context. This view offers a framework that can help us analyze the following stories connecting animal behavior with duty.

In March 2008, New Zealand conservation officials rushed to Mahia Beach off the northern coast to rescue two stranded whales. The surrounding area typically experiences about thirty stranded whales a year, so it was no surprise when the call came.[4] Two pygmy sperm whales, a mother and a calf, were distressed and confused as a nearby sandbar occluded their view of open water. When Malcolm Smith of the Mahia Beach Conservation Department arrived, he and his team worked feverishly for over an hour to try and get both whales to open ocean. No matter what he tried, the whales could not get a navigational bearing. Cold and exhausted, Mr. Smith's options were quickly running out. In a short time, both whales would have to be put down.

Within minutes of giving up hope, onlookers on the beach spotted a wild bottle-nosed dolphin arriving. He was known to the locals as Moko. She was a frequent visitor to the Mahia area and was known to play with the swimmers, even letting them take rides by holding her dorsal fin. Upon her arrival to the scene, Mr. Smith could hear Moko and the whales making contact. They were communicating through high-pitched whistles and clicks. Amazingly, within minutes the whales no longer appeared distressed as Moko led them along the beach and straight out to sea. The whales never returned. When Moko returned to the beach, Mr. Smith said, "*I shouldn't do this, I know. We are meant to remain scientific, but I actually went into the water with the dolphin and gave it a pat afterwards because she really did save the day.*" This rescue was the first recorded incident in history where a dolphin communicated with whales and saved them from an otherwise certain death.

What is so remarkable about this behavior is how Moko solved the dilemma through communication and not physical force. From stories dating back to the ancient Greeks, dolphins have been recorded assisting drowning people by pushing them to the surface. This is a natural and potentially instinctual function, as they do the same for other distressed dolphins as well as newborn young. Rather than push against the whales to lead them to safety, as Mr. Smith and his team were attempting to do, Moko negotiated a conversation with them—and a solution was presented in a language that they both could understand.

Could this have been an example of a sense of duty between species? Carol Howard, an expert in dolphin echolocation, asserts in her book *Dolphin Chronicles*:

> *Some critics argue that this helping behavior is purely instinctive; the dolphins don't "know" what they are doing when they come to the aid of another. That seems unlikely; given their capacity for learned behavior, the behavior is at least*

partially conscious and volitional. This behavior may be more often directed toward relatives or close associates, but it is by no means restricted to that. Such caregiving behavior may be an example of what's called reciprocal altruism.

Dolphins are likely to behave in altruistic ways because sociality is such a basic part of their lives and they are likely to need similar help at some point themselves—you're more likely to get help when you need it if you give it to others of your group when they need it. They seem to extend the principle beyond their immediate group, even beyond species boundaries.[5]

Webster's defines altruism as "the belief or practice of disinterested and selfless concern for the well-being of others."[6] Was Moko was exhibiting a duty to altruistic behavior? To better put this question into context, it is helpful to frame known dolphin behavior around not just other marine mammals but also humans.

Off the cost of California, surfers know dolphins are as prevalent as any other sea creature in the water. From kelp beds teeming with life to heavily populated coral reefs, the dolphins go there for food, community, and shelter from the open ocean.

In early 2007, Todd Endris was surfing an area as he had done almost daily for several years. With no visible warning, he was hit three times by a ten- to fourteen-foot great white shark. Mr. Endris reported that for a split second, the shark had clamped its massive jaws down on his leg, and the force of the hit vaulted them both out of the water.[7] With each successive hit, the surfer's injuries became more and more grave.

On the second bite, the shark shredded his back as he bit down on his torso. Since the surfboard was sandwiched between his chest and the shark's teeth, most of his vital organs were, fortunately, protected. The third hit had most of Mr. Endris's right leg down its throat. With the shark having a tight bite on his leg, he was able to beat on its head and kick it with his left leg. The shark let go for a brief moment, and that is when a pod of bottle-nosed dolphins raced in on the scene and encircled the surfer.

With his arms and one leg uninjured, Mr. Endris started paddling back to shore while being shielded from additional attacks by the shark. The dolphins saved him from what could have been the last and fatal hit. Six weeks and multiple surgeries later, he was well enough to go back into the water.[8]

In another amazing story of dolphin rescue, four lifeguards swam off the coast of New Zealand in late 2004 when they were rapidly approached by a pod of dolphins. Their aggressive speed startled the lifeguards as they had only reached the halfway point of their training session. The dolphins tightly encircled the swimmers, darting only inches away while slapping their flukes against the water.

For almost forty-five minutes this continued until the lead lifeguard drifted briefly from the others. A large dolphin appeared to become agitated and quickly dove deep in front of him. As he turned around to look to see where it went, he could see the silhouette of a great white shark beneath the surface about twelve feet away, headed toward the three women lifeguards. In a frantic display of splashes and flying fins, it was clear that the dolphins were protecting the swimmers from an attack. Until a rescue boat arrived, the dolphins were the only protection against the shark that never broke the surface of the water. The shark left promptly once the boat arrived, yet the dolphins stayed with the swimmers as they swam back to shore.[9]

In 2008, a Philippine tuna fisherman provided an account of his harrowing ordeal when a squall quickly overturned his small fishing boat. He claims to have floated for over twenty-four hours in cold and rough seas. While attempting to paddle on a piece of salvaged floating foam, he became exhausted. A nearby pod of dolphins and two whales, according to the government-investigated report, joined the fisherman, and the several dolphins began nudging him toward shore. At some point during his exhaustion, he fell unconscious and woke up on a nearby beach where locals were attending to him.[10]

Even Hollywood actor Dick Van Dyke, in a recent interview, told a story of his own rescue by porpoises. The then eighty-four-year-old actor had fallen asleep and drifted out to sea on his surfboard. He said, "*I woke up out of site of land, and I started paddling with the swells and I started seeing fins swimming around me and I thought, I'm dead. They turned out to be porpoises [and] they pushed me all the way to shore.*[11]

Besides the order that makes up dolphins and whales, called cetaceans, no other marine animal has ever been documented to show such a profound and widespread protective behavior of other species. When we attempt to interpret why this behavior exists, we find that the hypotheses are many but the conclusions are few. Since these marine mammals exhibit common behavioral tactics, like encircling an unprotected victim or pushing a drowning mammal to the surface, we might hypothesize that they are merely following simple preservation instincts.

Yet, the reasons why a dolphin, porpoise, or a whale might rescue another species still have not been fully explained. Some hypothesize that they do this out of a sense of reciprocity—where they might need to call in the same favor someday. Others believe that it is just a matter of being a good social steward to others in need. Still, it appears in light of current explanations that these mammals have an instinct of duty, and some of them have a disposition for altruistic behavior. If this is true, then the cetacean community is much more instinctive and yet cognitive than we ever thought possible.

Even though they may not have the same moral law that humans recognize, perhaps these mammals have their own. And perhaps they struggle to adhere to it just as we do. Though they might not be part of a Kantian argument for making decisions based on moral law, could these advanced creatures have their own rules for which they have an innate duty to be compliant? Without careful and diligent research in this area, it is a delicate challenge to responsibly avoid anthropomorphism, assigning human characteristics to something that is not human. Still, it is entirely feasible for an advanced creature capable of rationality to have developed a code of conduct that transcends generational and species variation. There is no doubt that we are only beginning to understand cetacean community behavior, social dynamics, problem-solving skills, and other abilities like altruism that put these creatures in a mental capacity above most other animals on the planet.

So while we must avoid projecting our own attributes on that of the intelligent marine life, we cannot deny the way they often interface with those in their own species, as well as those outside. This behavior is clear evidence of a sense of obligation to something beyond mere opportunity or reciprocal altruism. It is certainly possible that the complexity of how they make decisions is tied to a concept of duty beyond anything we can observe with clarity or are able currently to explain. Nonetheless, it unquestionably provides evidence of another common bond between animal and human.

The Human Dimension of Duty

The human dimension of duty is fascinating because we face its implications every day. When you drive up to an intersection with a four-way stoplight, you have the option to obey the law and stop like everyone else or disobey the law and run the light. What keeps you from disobeying the law? There is no barricade that comes down in front of you physically preventing you from running the light. There might also be no immediate retribution for your actions, provided that you don't cause an accident or pass a police officer that saw what you did. Though you might experience the penalty after the traffic camera takes your picture, it is entirely within your ability to obey or disobey the law temporarily at that one intersection.

Beneath any responsibility for someone to uphold the law (if nothing more than to avoid a traffic ticket), there is an innate disposition of duty that is communicating one's obligations to the situation. A person's disposition might be that he or she owes their family a safe return from a trip because their daughters need a healthy father. Or perhaps it is because we owe everyone else at an intersection the right to be at minimal risk to life, injury, and loss of property. Perhaps we owe everyone the ability to proceed through the intersection efficiently toward their destinations. It is mindboggling to ponder all of the elements that make up what happens at a simple stoplight. But the principle behind them all is clear. Our instinct of duty actively operates all the time—and we rarely know it is there.

English tort law originally formed the legal concept called duty of care, which establishes what duty individuals may have to each other to not suffer unreasonable harm or loss. If we were to take this simple principle and transpose it into our own families, teams, and organizations, what would it reveal? Would we see bonds of healthy relationships acting in the best interest of others? Would our duty uphold values and ideals that contribute to connectedness within these relationships? Whatever this unveiling might produce, it should at least perk our attention to the need for understanding our dispositions of duty.

Of course, not everyone has the same duty of care for the same people. Nevertheless, we all have a common underlying system that evaluates the complexities of our relationships and, in turn, shapes how we make decisions about those individuals. It forms our models and conclusions of relating to people. As social and political theorist Richard Bellamy states, *"Human beings are not born autonomous and self-supporting; they achieve this status through society. Our social duties are best seen as an acknowledgement of this fact."*[12]

We also have a duty to our social environment. Sometimes it is derived from our own dedication to a specific role in society. Consider Captain Chesley "Sully" Sullenberger who writes about successfully ditching US Airways Flight 1549 in the Hudson River, saving 155 passengers, in his book *Highest Duty: My Search for What Really Matters*. He says:

> *I am trained to be intolerant of anything less than the highest standards of my profession. I believe air travel is as safe as it is because tens of thousands of my fellow airline and aviation*

*workers feel a shared sense of duty to make safety
a reality every day. I call it a daily devotion to
duty. It's serving a cause greater than ourselves.[13]*

For Captain Sullenberger, his sense of duty is provided through his dedication to the safety of himself,
his equipment, and his passengers. The necessity for
this disposition in a pilot of an aircraft is not only an
intellectual attribute but also a direct requirement for
the survival of all those on board. As we reflect on the
duty we choose to exhibit to others, we should consider the role that we play in their lives. What impact does
our duty have on sustaining others' welfare? The only
way to answer this question is to be willing to look at
our circle of influence and the comprehensive effect
we have on those people.

In addition to what duty we choose inwardly, our
concept of duty can also be derived from our social environment. We build a collection of contributing forces through a lifetime of experiences, trust and distrust
in relationships, knowing the dependability or failure
of people who had owed duty to us, and knowing the
times we came through for someone who was in need
just as the times we abandoned others. Our history
and interpretations of it are stored and processed in
our instinct of duty. As such, how we act socially is determined by the way this dutiful behavior is displayed.

Sometimes our environment establishes what
duty should mean for us simply through a decree. In
the military context, the full embodiment of duty is
evident in the concept of the soldier. The U.S. Army

Leadership Manual states:

...duty extends beyond everything required by law, regulation, and orders. Professionals work not just to meet the minimum standard, but consistently strive to do their very best. Army leaders commit to excellence in all aspects of their professional responsibility... Part of fulfilling duty is to exercise initiative—anticipating what needs to be done before being told what to do...In rare cases, a leader's sense of duty also has to detect and prevent an illegal order. Duty requires refusal to obey it—leaders have no choice but to do what is ethically and legally right.[14]

The need to address a higher sense of calling or duty in the U.S. Army is said to have been promulgated with the outcome of the My Lai massacre, where an unlawful order led to the slaughter of hundreds of unarmed Vietnamese civilians.[15] Even within the context of the greater Vietnam War, the reality of this event shocked the upper echelon of the military as well as Congress and President Nixon. A greater purpose had to be communicated to soldiers even in light of the fact that the North Vietcong were recruiting women and children to carry out their attacks. There had to be a higher rule of law to protect the unarmed.

War is barbaric, but the U.S. realized that it was the duty of the professional soldier to fight the enemy and protect the innocent, and this duty included the right to disobey any unethical or illegal order. Prior to this event, there was no army paradigm for what a soldier was to do with an unlawful order. Even for Vietnam POWs, there was no written code or set beliefs that told a soldier how or why to resist.

Dating back to the British Charge of the Light Brigade against Russian forces in the Crimean War,[16] or even Gettysburg within the Civil War,[17] there were many military disasters that appeared to make little sense to the individuals in the midst of the battle. However, with a perceived duty to only follow orders, the results were often catastrophic.

After the decimation of My Lai, the army started dealing with the reality of lawful orders and a soldier's responsibility to a concept of "higher law." As SGM (ret.) Steven Carter discussed during an interview, "For the Army, the first such code or creed was the Ranger Code, for POW's it was the Code of Conduct, and in the early 2000s came the NCO (non-commissioned officer) creeds for various branches of service." Here is an excerpt of the U.S. Army NCO Creed:

I am aware of my role as a Noncommissioned Officer. I will fulfill my responsibilities inherent in that role. All soldiers are entitled to outstanding leadership; I will provide that leadership. I know my soldiers and I will always place their needs above my own. I will communicate consistently with my soldiers and never leave them uninformed. I will be fair and impartial when recommending both rewards and punishment. Officers of my unit will have maximum time to accomplish their duties; they will not have to ac-

*complish mine. I will earn their respect and con-
fidence as well as that of my soldiers. I will be
loyal to those with whom I serve; seniors, peers,
and subordinates alike. I will exercise initiative
by taking appropriate action in the absence of orders. I will not compromise my integrity, nor my
moral courage.*[18]

Last came the Warrior Ethos (which also became
a part of the Soldier's Creed) and says, "*I will always
place the mission first. I will never accept defeat. I will
never quit. I will never leave a fallen comrade.*"[19] As we
can see in these examples, the army recognizes the importance of a concept of a higher code, beyond what
could come from a single order, to which all orders
must be subservient. The duty of a soldier is to something greater than himself (universally) and to the orders of his superiors (locally). The universal code su-
persedes the local code when there is contention.

For other organizations, there is no manual de-
scribing how to define duty. In the private and professional sectors, for example, there are implications of
duty within mission statements, ethics programs, and
core values. For leaders within faith-based communities, duty is derived through the doctrine accepted by
the church—and is a key component to the actions
of a believer. From theology to liturgy, and from the
baptism of infants to funeral proceedings, everything
is contained within a greater transcendent duty. One
definition of duty published from a Christian leadership organization states:

Duty: That which a person owes to another; That to which a person is bound, by any natural, ethical, or legal obligation, to pay, do, or perform. Forbearance of that which is forbid by ethics, law, justice or propriety. It is our duty to refrain from lewdness intemperance, profaneness and injustice. Reverence, obedience and prayer to God are indispensable duties.[20]

The concept of duty is clearly not limited to the Christian faith; it is also found in Judaism's concept of the Law and the Prophets, Hindu's traditional and broadly-defined term for dharma, the Islamic concept to enjoin what is right and forbid what is wrong, as well as the social duties within Buddhism. For faith communities, duty is the inherent and transcendent commitment to the principles by which human life is to be conducted. It is a natural component of the social and theological infrastructure.

Whether we rely on our faith, our cultural values or an organization to which we belong, we still must reach down farther into the realm of why duty is so important. What we find at the base of this instinct is the reason for its existence in our lives: duty is the only way that valuable, sustainable relationships can exist. Occasionally, we understand what it means to fulfill and express our duty to others. Likewise, we are able to neglect our duties to others and fail to hold ourselves to the moral code we have adopted. It is these differences we find in the alpha and omega behavior of duty.

The Omega of Duty

When our disposition for duty is self-centric, the outcome can be disastrous. Like the instinct of self-preservation, the focus of our disposition of duty determines how beneficial we will be in leadership roles. When our sense of obligation is only to our own needs, then we are less aware of the needs of others. With this lack of awareness, we are unable to see others with the clarity needed to be decisive and strategic about the decisions we make on their behalf and for the good of the organization. For the omega, we are left to our own reflexive behavior and reflections we conjure up in our mind.

We are naturally born with a duty first to ourselves. Much of this behavior is due to our self-preservation instinct. Outside of any other context, we are selfish. However, over time there are many influences like family, community, faith, education, social dynamics, and so on that help to shape our behavior to a more balanced social norm. Still, when those influences no longer sufficiently offer a plausible reason to be dutiful to others, or when life events create a vacuum void of a need to be dutiful to others, we can slip into a more grandiose or entitlement-focused representation of ourselves—we create an image of ourselves that is narcissistic—of duty to the self alone. We lose a healthy sense of connectedness within the social realm. Renowned psychotherapist Alexander Lowen once said regarding the impact that narcissism has on who we are:

The denial of feeling characteristic of all narcissists is most manifest in their behavior toward others. They can be ruthless, exploitative, sadistic, or destructive to another person because they are insensitive to the other's suffering or feeling. This insensitivity derives from insensitivity to one's own feelings. Empathy, the ability to sense other people's moods or feelings, is a function of resonance. We can feel another person's sadness because it makes us feel sad; we can share another's joy because it evokes good feelings in us. But if we are incapable of feeling sadness or joy, we cannot respond to these feelings in another person, and we may even doubt that they have such feelings. When we deny our feelings, we deny that others feel.

Only on this basis can we explain the ruthless behavior of some narcissists like the corporate executives who drive their employees remorselessly and create a reign of terror by their indifference to human sensibilities and indiscriminate firings, without regard for people's feelings...

Narcissism splits the reality of an individual into accepted and rejected aspects, the latter being projected, then, upon others...For example, the con man who thinks of himself as shrewd and superior must see his victim as gullible and stupid.[21]

The danger of this disconnectedness is clear. When our minds are producing and projecting images that are the antithesis of reality, then we have the propensity to lose objectivity. We do not cooperate in leadership with our followers. We do not collaborate with our peers. We are lone, omega creatures due to our own mental isolation. We can be sensitive to criticism, poor listeners, have a lack of empathy, a distaste for mentoring, and an intense desire to compete.[22]

Following the aggressive acts by North Korea during a 2010 torpedoing of a South Korean ship and conducting an artillery barrage on an island in a disputed border area, the dictatorship of Kim Jon Il has come under greater scrutiny. Despite international outcry over his confrontational stance, even from other communist countries, his actions are as concerning as they are enigmatic.

Whether a calculating authoritarian or a tyrannical narcissist or both, the rhetoric he transmits to the rest of the world reveals highly localized duty to his constructed idea of the North Korean state. This says nothing of a duty to the people of that country. According to Amnesty International, crippling food shortages exacerbated by the government economic policies have caused widespread illness as thousands are forced to survive on eating grass and tree bark.[23]

Additionally, an organization called North Korean Economy Watch put together a collection of satellite photos showing the luxurious accommodations used by government officials in light of recent news of dangerous poverty that now pervades the country.[24] As time goes on, there will be a greater and greater challenge for North Korea to remain fortressed from the inquiries, critique, and reaction of the world. Nonetheless, the pressure that currently is being placed on the authoritarian regime from world figures is revealing characteristics that give us insight into its leader's disposition of duty.

According to Gary Yukl's research in *Leadership in Organizations*, he explains how narcissists have a number of characteristic flaws:

> *[Leaders] surround themselves with subordinates who are loyal and uncritical. They make decisions without gathering adequate information about the environment. In the belief that they alone are sufficiently informed and talented to decide what is best, objective advice is not sought or accepted from subordinates and peers. They tend to undertake ambitious, grandiose projects to glorify themselves, but in the absence of an adequate analysis of the situation, the projects are likely to be risky and unrealistic.*
>
> *When a project is not going well, they tend to ignore or reject negative information, thereby missing the opportunity to correct problems in time to avert disaster. When failure is finally evident, the narcissist leader refuses to admit any responsibility, but instead finds scapegoats to blame. Finally, because they exploit the organization to compensate their own sense of inadequacy, extreme narcissists are unable to plan for an orderly succession of leadership. They see*

themselves as indispensable and cling to power,
in contrast to emotionally mature executives
who are able to retire gracefully when their job is
done and it is time for new leadership.[25]

Duty is fed by our concept of obligation and commitment, and it is to whom our disposition of duty is targeted that will determine our disposition to this instinct. If our disposition is built on the reinforcement of a secluded worldview, then shall our perspectives and actions. Because of this unhealthy capability we have for isolation, we need to learn to be reflective rather than reflexive leaders. However, reflection can't occur within the dark isolation cells of our mind. Instead, we must reflect on who we are in relation to something else—objective reality, outside resources, other people, and contexts of truth that lie outside our own reductionist tendencies. Only through connectedness to truth outside our own mind, in the realm of the alpha of duty, can we find the tools we need to have a duty for others.

The Alpha of Duty

Joe was twenty-two and just out of college. Since he was the only college graduate to apply for the job, his boss was willing to make him a manager over twelve people. Joe wasn't getting paid very much, and he knew his staff was receiving even less. For the first year, he and his team were amazingly fortunate and the right answers to boost production each quarter fell right in their laps. It couldn't have been an easier first year for the new manager. However, although Joe's department was doing very well and had received accolades from the executive wing, the company overall was struggling.

As a result, the CEO announced that year-end bonuses would likely be canceled company-wide. Morale among the departments took a big hit. Joe knew that the only reason his team performed so well was because they felt an ongoing duty to exceed their numbers and show the rest of the company how dedicated they were. Yet the bonuses were always something to which everyone looked forward.

One day the CEO walked up to Joe and handed him a corporate bank check. "*What is this for?*" Joe asked. "*It's the manager's bonus. All managers get one based on their team's individual performance.*" Jim's salary wasn't great, but it was able to meet his needs. The bonus money would be a step to knocking down his student loans, but there was a higher principle here that kept nagging him. Something he had seen the previous day outside the office had made up his mind. "*I am going to give it to my staff,*" Joe said. The CEO smiled, "*Do whatever you think is best, Joe.*"

At his next staff meeting, the team was looking forlorn. Tired from late hours and the knowledge that there was no bonus coming, they had little enthusiasm for sitting in a conference room. Joe walked in and sat down, "*Folks, you worked hard the first three quarters of this year. And I know that corporate has said that you would not be getting bonuses, but I want to offer you a small thank you for all that you have done."* There were many puzzled looks, but most assumed it would be small gift cards to the coffee cart on the first floor.

Brenda, a single woman with a child in daycare, sighed and said, *"Thanks, Joe, you have always taken good care of us."* She liked Joe, and she knew that he was only doing what he could. But there was no way that a coffee gift card would help at all. Joe smiled, *"I can't provide you what you are worth to this company right now, but I will do what little I can."* He handed out twelve envelopes and asked everyone to open them right then. Some jumped out of their chairs and cheered; others were giving him handshakes and bear hugs. The day before, Jim had cashed his bonus at the bank and then asked for twelve cashier's checks in the amount of $1,000 each.

Brenda opened her envelope and just sat in her chair sobbing. She felt a hand touch her shoulder. *"Are you alright?"* Joe asked. She responded, *"I had to choose whether to get my car fixed or pay for daycare. My only option was to start taking the bus with my daughter and drop her off on the ride to work. The car repairs came to $858."* She started crying again. Joe gently squeezed her shoulder and smiled. For the past month he had seen Brenda walk across the street from the bus stop to the office, often on rainy Seattle days. Every time he saw her, he had meant to ask her what had happened to her car, but he got sidetracked. With each day, she looked more and more exhausted.

When the CEO handed Joe the check, it was clear that no matter Brenda's situation, this was the right time to do something for her—for each of them. He felt a duty that transcended his duties as manager. Word had gotten around to other managers that somehow Jim's team had received bonuses. Many knew Joe personally and figured the only way this could have happened was through his dedication to his team. In response, the other managers did the same and gave their bonuses to their teams. Morale had increased so much that the next week everyone's teams were competing to outperform each other in sales of their products for the final quarter of the year. They ended up posting a fourth quarter profit that shocked investors and, as a result, their stock rose by 34%. By the end of January, they moved up the Fortune 500 list and were seemingly unstoppable.

Late one afternoon the CEO walked by Joe's office. He said, "*I have something for you, Joe*" and gave him a Hallmark card. Joe opened it, and it read, "*Thanks for taking care of those under your care. This one is just for you, Joe. We'll take care of bonuses from now on.*" It was signed by all of the board of directors. Included in the card was a check for $12,000 and a company stock options certificate for 1,000 shares.

As we can learn from this story, Joe had a crisis of duty. He evaluated the benefit to himself and his duty to the people that helped him succeed his first year as a manager. His crisis was short-lived because he already had a predisposition of gratefulness for such a hard-working staff. In the book *Good to Great,* author Jim Collins refers to these types of people as Level 5 leaders. They are not always charismatic and self-assured. Instead, they build enduring greatness through a paradoxical blend of personal humility and professional will.[26]

As we can see, great leaders are not about narcissistic dominance so often seen in omega behavior. They are instead dedicated to transcendent principles that shape community and purpose. Their decisions are constructive and nurture the health of the organization, rather than tear it down. Inherently, their sense of duty is based on their sense of purpose, which is not for themselves.

In Margaret Wheatley's book *Turning to One Another: Simple Conversations to Restore Hope to the Future,* she says:

> *Even if we don't use the word vocation, most of us want to experience a sense of purpose to our lives. From a young age, and especially as we mature, people often express the feeling of life working through them, of believing there's a reason for their existence. I always love to hear a young person say that they know there's a reason why they're here. I know that if they can hold onto that sense of purpose, they'll be able to deal with whatever life experiences await them. If we don't feel there's a meaning to our lives, life's difficulties can easily overwhelm and discourage us.*

This sense of a purpose beyond ourselves is a universal human experience, no matter our life circumstance. We don't have to be comfortable, well-fed, or safe in order to feel purpose in our lives. Often those in the most terrible circumstances of imprisonment or poverty are the best teachers. How they endure tragedy and suffering gives us the clearest insight into what it means to have a vocation to be fully human.[27]

From our story, Joe could have felt entitled to the bonus. Yet, his natural reaction was based on a transcendent purpose to help nurture the efforts and relationships of those he led. He had a purpose beyond his vocation, and it was a principle that went beyond his own comfort. His reason for being in leadership was the people he led. His duty was based on transcendent beliefs about what was right, and this duty prompted making choices for the greater good.

Duty is like a safety line we give to someone else. Once we hand it to them and they clip it to their safety harness, it is an unbreakable contract of dependability. They should never question the safety or reliability of what they have entrusted to our care. This duty contract can be the love and respect in a family, the dedication of a provider of financial or moral support, the commitment of a hard-working employee to a company, the handshake of a fellow soldier on the battlefield, or the loyalty a leader shows to his or her organization.

A leader's duty is to people. When we go to work, we work for them. When we make decisions, we make decisions for them. If every leader walked through his or her day in such a frame of mind, then much of our behavior, families, and ultimately our organizations, would change for the better.

Our instinct of duty has certain inertia behind it already in the form of a disposition, and our actions early in life typically reveal an obligation only to ourselves. It takes effort to change directions, but as mature adults we have a responsibility to be dutiful to one another.

We also have a responsibility to question if we are expressing the duty of care that is needed. If we could step into a family member's, or one of our subordinate's, shoes, we should be able to see a duty of care unique to our relationship with them. Finally, we must know the belief systems that shape our concept of duty. They are the binding force that many of our other decisions coalesce around. Many influences have created our individual concepts of duty. For the sake of our organizations, we need to have the clearest understanding of how our duty impacts our decisions. People are depending on us to take this seriously.

In Ken Blanchard and Phil Hodges's work *Lead Like Jesus: Lessons for Everyone From the Greatest Leadership Role Model of All Time*, they assert:

There are two kinds of people. Those that are driven and those that are called. Driven people think they own everything. They own their relationships. They own their possessions. They own their position. As a result they spend most of their time protecting what they own. Everything they do is determined by their own self-interest. And so if they praise you or encourage you, they're really doing it for their own good. Called people, on the other hand, think everything in life is on loan. Their relationships are on loan. Their possessions are on loan. Their position is on loan. As a result, they are not defensive or protective about their position as a leader. In fact, if a better leader comes along, they will partner with that person—sometimes even step aside and take a different role—because the only reason they are leading is to serve other people.[28]

We have to ask ourselves if we feel called or driven to be a leader. Is the duty that we embrace also including the duty to always do what is in the best interest of others or the organization, even if it includes taking ourselves away from a role we are no longer fit for? Sometimes the hardest component to duty is the self-denial of our own pride. As we come to the end of our journey into the instinct of duty and move on to the instinct of hope, let us pause and reflect on the final words penned by then commander-in-chief George Washington in his 1783 resignation letter to Congress:

I consider it an indispensable duty to close this last solemn act of my official life, by commending the interests of our dearest country to the protection of Almighty God, and those who have the superintendence of them, to his holy keeping. Having now finished the work assigned to me, I retire from the great theatre of action; and bidding an affectionate farewell to this August body under whose orders I have so long acted, I here offer my commission, and take my leave of all the employments of public life.[29]

Principles for Reflection

• We often associate duty with organizations like the military or other government agencies. However, duty is needed in all organizations. Does it exist in yours?

• Part of our lack of interest in duty is because our organizations typically do not exemplify commitment. They only offer compensation. As leaders, how can we change this perception?

• Our instinct of duty will instigate our behavior for making decisions as leaders. Likewise, our followers will mimic the duty we express. What if everyone in your organization had your disposition for duty?

• Duty is not about responding to expectations. It is an offering we give others after thoroughly pondering what we should do and what we are able to do.

• Every day is an opportunity to show our duty of care. Those that depend on us should always be able to tug on that lifeline and know that it is there.

• What situations and people in our past and present influence how we view duty? What positive or negative impact do they have on our disposition today?

7. HOPE

"Most of the important things in the world have been accomplished by people who have kept on trying when there seemed to be no hope at all."

—Dale Carnegie

"Dum spiro spero." (When I breathe, I hope.)

—Cicero

We have seen how instincts are complex instigators of behavior, and as we recondition ourselves to new ways of behavior, we shape these instincts. This conditioning is an effort of reflection—not from within the isolation of our own thoughts but in a unified survey of who we are in our environment. Likewise, we have also seen that when we fail to make intentional steps for change, we are still vulnerable to change from outside influences. If we don't shape our untamed instincts, they will shape us.

As we embark on the last instinct of untamed leadership—hope—we need to pause and reflect on the cohesion that exists between them all. It is presently controversial to say that hope is an instinct. In the definitive sense, it is an instigator of behavior, true, because a presence or lack of hope clearly shapes response modes within our brains and thus, our actions too. Yet, from a psychological or ethological perspective, scientific research has produced little results and has made little effort to conclude that it is an innate function—like self-preservation, for example. Using the commonly accepted psychological definition that hope is the ability to plan pathways to desired goals despite obstacles, and agency or motivation to use these pathways,[1] we find little basis from which to conclude that hope is pre-formed and existent at birth. Most research indicates that hope is a developmental component derived as we pass from infancy up through adolescence.[2] In the animal behavior realm, the literature is practically void of established experiments, research, or conclusions that might imply that animals have hope. So, where does that leave the instinct of hope?

To answer this question, we need to first see hope in its proper context. It is an instigator of behavior and yet it responds to outside environmental influences like any of the other instincts. We are disposed to hope depending on how it has been developed over our lifetime. Some people are disposed to be hopeful regardless of the circumstances, whereas others must be convinced or coerced to have hope.

Hope can be reflexive—as in the spontaneous hope generated from a charismatic leader. Hope can also be reflective—as in the hope provided in our faith. It can be derived from a sense of purpose or level of confidence we might have in a certain outcome outside our control. Hope is built upon a template within our minds to know what hope is. Although we use it to establish things like self-identity, and most importantly how relationships and communities function, we still struggle to make sense of it. We know when hope is present, and we most certainly know when it is vacant from our lives. As Walter Fluker writes in his book *Ethical Leadership: The Quest for Character, Civility, and Community*:

> *[Hope] in reality is the driving force of all human relations. Without hope, individuals and groups plunge into despair. When despair informs practice, desperate people do desperate things! Businesses, organizations, and nations that are bereft of hope are doomed to fail because people need to know that the future is not predetermined; that they can make a difference that will affect outcomes. Hope has a tenacity of vision. It refuses to yield when confronted with despair because it dares to see beyond the present and to work toward the envisioned future with all its challenges and ambiguities. The greatest of leaders are those who inspire hope for change and transformation and then guide others in the implementation of the vision.*[3]

As we explore the instinct of hope, we will see how we are wired to have hope in our lives. We use it and need it all the time. When it is seemingly absent, then every other instinct we have suffers. When we have great hope in something tangible, then the other instincts thrive. As a result, hope is not something we merely learn later in life. The template for it must exist within us from the beginning. Though it might be developed over the course of our lives, it is formed from something that is raw and integral to our very nature.

Beyond Mere Animal Instinct

Hope isn't easy to find in the raw instincts of animals. Thus, we have to question if we believe we are observing it in animals, whether or not we are merely projecting a human understanding, scientific or otherwise, of what we think hope-filled behavior might look like. Such is the ongoing and complex debate of anthropomorphism. Human beings naturally struggle to minimize or negate our biases and human-centric interpretations when it comes to animal behavior, yet we are inexorably tied to them both. We cannot disassociate ourselves from our humanity to look at animals from any other context. As Michael Bavidge and Ian Ground state in *Can We Understand Animal Minds?*:

First of all, if anyone thinks that the only way to understand what it is like to be a lion is to be a lion, then the only way for us to arrive at such understanding would be to become lions. But this must strike us as a logically insurmountable obstacle. It is to say that understanding lions is a destination that human beings could never reach. But even ignoring this problem, even if, per impossible [sic], we could become lions, a further hazard may prevent us from completing our journey. Many creatures, we may believe, perhaps including lions, do not have the intelli-

gence to understand much about what it is like to be them.[4]

When we look at animals in hopes of observing hope, we must first examine how we can know anything of emotional value. Jeffrey Moussaieff Masson and Susan McCarthy eloquently address the delicate issue of studying animal behavior and emotions in their book *When Elephants Weep: The Emotional Lives of Animals*:

> *Short of being another person, there is no way to know with certainty what another person feels, although few people, even philosophers, carry their solipsism (the belief that the self can know nothing but the self) this far. In learning others' feelings, people are not always led by words alone, but watch behavior—gestures, the face, the eyes—patterns and consistency over time. Conclusions are based on this, and ground everyday life decisions. We love certain people, hate others, trust some, fear others, and act on this basis. Belief in the emotions of others is indispensable to live in human society.*[5]

From a human perspective, we depend on our own context of experience and self-knowledge to shape our understanding of others. No one person has ever experienced your feeling of thirst, yet through your understanding of thirst, you can better understand the thirst of another. In a similar context, when we look at animals, we cannot neglect the obvious links we have to common emotional experiences and our interpretations of those experiences. As Chantek states in *Anthropomorphism, Anecdotes, and Animals*:

How can you raise an ape in a human environment, provide human experiences, and encourage human behavior, such as language acquisition or comprehension, to make the ape more humanlike, and then succeed in being nonanthropomorphic [sic] in your interpretations?[6]

Chantek's statement brings to light the intrinsic dilemma about interpreting animal behavior. There is no agreed upon parameter that allows behaviorists to determine when to value human-based interpretations of animal behavior and when not to. So, we must explore the possibility of hope in animals with guarded optimism.

Helpful guides for this discussion come from the following animal stories. During their research on whales, Elin Kelsey and Doc White met up with Sandy Lanham, the pilot and founder of Environmental Flight Services, a nonprofit organization that provides research flights for biologists in Mexico. During one of their interviews, Ms. Lanham said:

I have seen instances with gray whales, when the airplane would scare them. The calf would hurry back to her mother, and the mother would stretch her pectoral flipper to just gently brush the calf. We're always cautioned against reading emotion into wildlife; there's a reluctance to ascribe feelings to whales. But the thing is, what

other binding factor is there except for emotions?
What else is going to ensure a mother takes care
of her young?[7]

Lanham's position is not rare among a growing number of ethologists and comparative psychologists. Rather than holding to classical assertions dating back to the eighteenth and nineteenth centuries, many see that animal emotion, while a delicate topic today, is one of extreme importance in understanding what animals think and experience in any similar context to that of humans. When speaking of hope, there is growing evidence to suggest how emotions have a deep interconnectedness with other emotions. So, to ignore one emotional response and accept another poses challenging discontinuity. Mary Midgley affirms this assertion in *Animals and Why They Matter*:

> *The terms hope and hopeful are in fact quite regularly used about animals, not just by idiots, but by careful and systematic observers of animal behaviour. They are not used out of sentimental projection, but because they are needed to describe one important sector of the normal range of moods displayed – a sector no less important in other animals than in man. Hope is surely on the same footing as fear.*[8]

While we cannot take the brash and irresponsible step and contend that animals are identical to human beings in the emotions or mental responses they experience, we can make the case that there is some form of commonality. It is certainly a valid assertion to state that some animals could have a different form of the same emotions that humans might have. The fact that they cannot communicate that emotion does not make it an undiscoverable black box. If nothing else, the possibility of similar brain structure between certain animals and humans should cause us to recognize the enigma of this behavior and prompt ongoing research. We should be looking to see whether or not these similarities are functionally equivalent. The same is true of the possibility of animals experiencing a sense of hope. Masson and McCarthy conclude their examination of animal hope by saying:

> *Wittgenstein [the German philosopher] argues that only those who have mastered the use of language can hope. Not only does this statement remain unproven to this day, but there seems no good reason to doubt that an animal can imagine or even possibly dream about the future. Animals may lack the language of hope, but the feelings that underlie it are probably shared by humans and animals alike. If animals can remember and dream about the past, if fear can be relived, why can they not imagine and project a future in which fear will be unnecessary?*[5]

We commonly accept that hope is nothing more than a feeling of expectation and desire for a certain thing to happen. Based on the context we have discussed so far, it is reasonable to argue that an animal capable of feeling emotions might also be expressing them in ways to which we are blinded. For example, in the book *Of Wolves and Men*, Barry Lopez states:

> *[An] aerial hunter, trapping on the ground one year, caught a large male black wolf in one of his traps. As he approached, the wolf lifted his trapped foot, extended it toward him, and whined softly.*

This wolf was wild and more than likely had only negative experiences when it came to humans in his environment. Thus, the wolf would have had no other association from which to judge that another animal or person could free it from a trap. What intrinsic ability would this wolf have for assuming that a human could help him—unless there was a sense of expectation or a desire? Furthermore, the natural disposition that should have taken over would have been one of self-preservation from a human that was approaching it. Even in its wounded and pained state, the injured wolf should have growled or made efforts to flee. Instead, it processed the situation and made a choice to relinquish any other instinctual inclination and supersede them all with an expression, a desire, for help.

Taking this a step further, for the wolf to deny all other innate preservation instincts and rely on hope alone would mean that it had to innately and cognitively go against thousands of years of behavioral disposition. The wolf had to change its own disposition of hope to include the possibility of being helped by the hunter. By raising its paw and whimpering in a self-deprecating manner, the wolf took on a role that would have been foreign to itself as the chief predator in its environment. This appears to be supporting evidence of a wild animal who entirely altered its sense of identity in one moment of desire to live. This was not a component of self-preservation but one of hope beyond itself.

Researchers are now looking at the complex, controversial, and misunderstood science of emotion within animals. As such, the documented stories that are currently few, are growing. The importance of this research is that it has a goal not of humanizing animals, but instead of finding ways to examine them on their own terms. Still, the functional reality of animal instincts invigorates us to better study ourselves. As we move away from the centuries of scientists who claim that animals feel no pain or express no emotion, we continually stand in a better position to understand our own expressions of emotion. Though we can never know undeniably that animals experience what humans do, we can make the effort to find out what it means to be animal-like, just like we seek to know what it means to be human.

The Human Dimension of Hope

Positive psychology is the scientific study of hope, and, although a young branch of the more established realm of classical human behavior, it is maturing and developing an area that has been relatively ignored in the understanding of the brain. Much of what we read within this grouping varies from scientific, academic, and medical approaches of restoring people to neutral or positive emotional states. Conversely, spheres of positive psychology have become more accessible to the public through individuals promoting neuro-linguistic programming (NLP) and neuro-associative conditioning (NAC), which are methods to alter thinking and behavior. Regardless of how we utilize hope for modifying behavior, we need to understand that hope exists, and, by consequence, humans rely on it to exist.

Until 2002, there were few descriptions of how hope might be an established component of our psyche and how it might help us derive outcomes based on goal-setting efforts. But as further research was done, more observations necessary to build a theory of hope came to fruition.

C.R. Snyder, Kevin Rand, and David Sigmon are credited with establishing Hope Theory both in name and concept. Essentially, they posit that hope is about the pathways from which goals elicit cognitive behavior.[9] This is an important aspect of understanding the goal-oriented side of the mind. Previously, where traditional perspectives on positive psychology were all based on the principle that the environment affected a person's behavior, newer theories now support human behavior as having both a greater reflective role and environmental role.

Reversing the relationship, transcendent behaviors better explain the creative and transforming activities within organizations today. In their research, Thomas Bateman and Christine Porath write:

...transcendent behaviors in the workplace are different from most other behaviors. Consistent with the defining feature of surpassing limiting factors, transcendent behavior at work is evidenced when people effect extraordinary change by exceeding demands, eliminating or overcoming constraints, and creating or seizing opportunities...

Such behavior serves the increasing need to be not victims or mere survivors of change but to create constructive, high-impact change.[10]

Hope is a transcendent behavior which simply keeps us moving ahead, when there is no other motivation to do so. It is something that we point to as a reference but can't quite explain. Like the Chinese proverb: *"Hope is what you find in the woods when there was nothing before. But as the people began walking in the same place, there appeared the path."*

Among the other untamed instincts, within the context of human leadership, hope is the only one that appears to initiate change in all of them. When we look at self-preservation, mimicry, communication, causality, rationality, and duty, within each of them there is a taproot to some form of hope.

For example, we seek to survive due to the inherent hope for a long and meaningful life for those we wish to preserve, and this translates to a need for value within our organizations. We pretend and mimic each other with a hope of being or becoming someone beyond our current vision of ourselves. We communicate because connectedness is bound to the hope of not being alone. We have an instinct for causality that is based on a hope for comprehending and affirming our model of how we lead, how our organization functions, and the accuracy of our worldview. Our instinct of rationality embraces a hope that what is seemingly enigmatic or irrational in our lives can be explained regardless of assertions to the contrary. Lastly, we have duty to one another, because we have a hope that by imputing our sense of support and sustainability to others, we are contributing to a greater good that is beyond our own experience or individual contribution.

The culmination of all leadership instincts is based on an innate need for hope. This is an important revelation in that every other instinct, while having the ability to be shaped and honed to specific forms of behavior, does not necessarily possess the heartbeat needed to drive every form of behavior. In that context, hope is critically important, and perhaps it is the one instinct that was created to instigate all other structures of human capacity. Certainly within the leadership realm, it is one of the most communicated and often abstract concepts that we use to motivate others' behavior. And as we have seen previously, unfortunately, the opposite also exists.

The Omega of Hope

It seems natural to talk about leadership and hope together. Yet, there is the strong likelihood that at least one leader will cross our paths that is the complete opposite. This person will knock us off balance, and we will spend enormous amounts of time feeling disturbed by what they say and do. We will struggle to establish predictable norms, and our outlook on many facets of our life might change. A job or career that was once an enjoyable, rewarding, and peaceful experience now suddenly feels like one where we are weathering the crests and troughs of a tumultuous sea. Feeling unable to navigate to any place of certainty, survival becomes the only goal. This is what omegas can do to their followers—crush their sense of hope.

A leader with this disposition is oblivious to the needs of his or her followers. Their instinct has been reshaped by negative experiences, or reactions to other situations, that have reinforced their suppression of a healthy and positive outlook. Their inner turmoil becomes our inner turmoil, as one cannot be without a sense of hope and yet still project hope to others. Taken to an extreme, leaders that nurture a vacancy of hope and foster despair will create a gravitational pull from which few will escape.

Despite the vast amount of literature on the disturbing psychology of Adolf Hitler, evidence of his vitriol and sadistic neuroses is extremely well-documented in the stories of his victims. His extermination of Jews during World War II is unfathomable. However, what is even more beyond our ability to understand is the extent to which despair permanently altered the hearts and souls of adults and children who witnessed these atrocities. The vortex of this regime was not just an absence of hope. Hitler sought out hope and eviscerated it. Marion Kaplan writes in her book, *Between Dignity and Despair: Jewish Life in Nazi Germany*:

> *One woman who was hopeless about her plight and fearful of becoming a burden on strangers, appealed to her husband to consider a joint suicide. Forlorn that both her children had emigrated, depressed that she had lost her home, and terrified of being arrested, she proposed: "We should...separate ourselves forever from this world by throwing ourselves...into the Neckar [river]." The husband argued against suicide for the time being, and each promised that if either committed suicide it would only be with the other. The husband's arrest, for a technical detail related to their packed furniture, drove the wife to despair, and she killed herself. Before turning on the gas, she wrote to her husband and children, asking their forgiveness. "Please try to understand me. I am desperate, crushed without hope. I can't continue to breathe. I am afraid of the prison walls which await me...Forgive me that I leave you like this. I am powerless...My heart is tearing apart. I am perspiring with fright day and night."[11]*

Even children that were secretly housed, smuggled across the borders, or sent via train outside the reach of Nazi SS troops were not insulated from a sense of hopelessness. Allan Zullo and Mara Bovsun write of eight-year-old Luncia Gamzer who was given reluctant sanctuary by a neighbor in her parents' community after the Nazis took notice of her Jewish family. They write:

For the first few days, Luncia sobbed because she was so miserable, sitting there in the corner, no toy to play with, no book to read . . . Mrs Szczygiel told Luncia, "You're lucky to be in my house, so stop your weeping." From then on, Luncia made sure that no one ever saw her cry. She would sob into a hanky, and then dry it under the bed. While that one was drying, she would weep into her other hanky. After one particularly bad crying jag, she told herself, Now I can't cry for a while because both hankies are wet. When they get dry, I can cry again.[12]

The effect of a vortex of despair is debilitating, and without a goal or a purpose, we have nothing to hope for in multiple aspects of our lives. We have no reason to take another step or make another decision. We disconnect from the resources from which we all need to function. We unwind the fabric that unites families, communities, and organizations simply through a lack of hope. We disconnect and disengage ourselves from the resources that we need and those that depend on us. A 2001 Gallup study estimated that individuals that were disconnected from their jobs were costing the U.S. economy between $292 and $355 billion a year. These amounts come from a survey that revealed 19% of workers are disengaged, tend to be significantly less productive, report being less loyal to their companies, are less satisfied with their personal lives, and are more stressed and insecure about their work than their colleagues. The study claimed that one in five people at your office is likely disengaged.[13]

What no leader should intentionally do is deny hope to those he or she leads. No leader should unintentionally deny hope to those he or she leads. It must not happen. What we as leaders experience, think, and believe will be projected to those that follow us. As a natural outcome, our own disengagement from our organizations will produce disengagement in our followers. Yet, there is hope in what can be done to instill hope in others. We must seize it within ourselves first. When leaders find hope is low for those who depend on them, they must seek it out, and when hope is full, leaders must pass it on.

The Alpha of Hope

In late 1984, President Ronald Reagan held a rally in St. Louis, Missouri, to garner a last push before the November election which was only days away. In this speech, he specifically addressed the younger generation of voters and rallied their hope for a safe country where they would only be limited by their own ability to dream. He said:

My generation and, well, a few generations between mine and yours, we have a sacred trust. We grew up in an America in which we just took it for granted that you could dream and make your dreams come true, if you are willing to go for them—that this was a land of opportunity, and it was denied to no one. Well, our sacred trust is, my generation and those of others I mentioned, to see that when it comes time to turn over to you young people the reins of this country, we're going to turn over to you an America that is free in a world at peace and in which you can dream and make your dreams come true.[14]

One of the obvious initiatives toward Reagan's idea of world peace was to break the rule of communism and the influence that nuclear proliferation was having on other superpowers. As a result, the U.S. nurtured what was already happening in the Soviet empire—the collapse of its communist ideology. The dismantling of the Iron Curtain quickly spread to neighboring countries, and a foreign sense of freedom came to permeate society. In Poland, Lech Walesa, the founder of the Solidarity movement who facilitated the breaking of communist strongholds in Eastern and Western Europe, said about Reagan, *"We in Poland . . . owe him our liberty."*[15]

In 1987, President Reagan traveled to West Berlin and delivered a bold and tenacious speech at the Brandenburg Gate calling on the General Secretary of the Communist Party of the Soviet Union. He said, *"General Secretary Gorbachev, if you seek peace, if you seek prosperity for the Soviet Union and Eastern Europe, if you seek liberalization: Come here to this gate! Mr. Gorbachev, open this gate! Mr. Gorbachev, tear down this wall!"*[16] If you were there in person or watching it on television, it took no effort at all to appreciate what Reagan's words were about to do for Europe. Hope, which had been suppressed for generations, had suddenly been injected back into the fabric of this fractured society. As political prisoners were released, they freely spoke about their experiences and the hope that ensued when they got word of Reagan's speech. Much of the world soon experienced the joy and responsibility that comes with democracy—all because of hope.

We can see in the events impacting the world how hope is constantly changed and is consistently challenged. Yet, for some reason, hope is integrated tightly within the scope of humanity, surviving beyond seemingly insurmountable odds. Margaret Wheatley writes of a story about a pregnant Rwandan mother of six whose village was destroyed by a massacre:

> She was shot first, buried under the bodies of each of her six slain children, and left for dead. She dug herself out, buried her children, bore her new child, and, soon thereafter, chose to adopt five children whose parents had been killed in the same massacre. She expressed her belief that her life had been spared so that she might care for these orphaned children after losing her own.[17]

There is a difference between hope that is destroyed and hope that overcomes. People look at the challenges they face and look to hope for new opportunities. Stories of hope are evident in many of the tragedies which have occurred over the last decade. We experienced the live footage of the twin towers on 9/11, we read of the genocide in Darfur and the poverty and hunger in Somalian cities plagued with clans stealing resources from their citizens to feed their own armies. Today we battle the policies and opinions of illegal immigration along America's southern border with seemingly no good answers. We watch mighty giants of industry dissolve along with our investment accounts over unscrupulous behavior at the executive level. We debate over federal answers to community issues and look at our elected leaders with the contempt of a sleuth of bears in a giant honey pot. We want hope in our world, and yet there are so many grave examples to the contrary. Still, what is innate to the human spirit cannot be contained, and we strive to create hope where it didn't previously exist.

A youth-focused leadership development program in Kenya called The Mbegu Trust is making a massive impact on the educational investments of Kenyan children. By building schools, advanced learning curriculums, and a mechanism within the community to turn leaders back to local issues, Mbegu is making generational investments. Recently they sponsored an essay contest on the topic of "The Leadership We Need to Build The Kenya and Africa We Want." Among the eight finalists was a seventeen-year-old girl whose essay title was "Fact Is, There is No Black Messiah." The young student writes:

The illusion that we await the chosen one, a legendary black Messiah, is but an excuse for our laziness to sit around and murmur about what is not working... believe that the unique force that drove Nelson Mandela to battle on for more than twenty-seven years lies within us all. It is not a supernatural energy from a mystical place. It is that hope for something better, the piercing eyes of a starving child and the cry of a bereaved mother, the desire for change, a better change. That is the force that should drive a leader.[18]

Having seen suffering personally since she was a child and yet to be able to express the foundational element of hope that exists in all of us is nothing short of visionary. This young leader sees the opportunity, and she knows what to do about it. Hope is her rally cry, and others will join her and build a revolutionary community that is immune from the types of fractured history that made up her childhood. Considering her turning her education back toward the ears and minds of the people in her community, she comes across as more qualified to speak on the topic of hope than many of us in leadership roles today.

As we look to our resources, and those who depend on us as leaders, we should have an equally fervent desire to establish hope. This is not a hope necessary to win an election or the rhetoric necessary to stir people's emotions alone. This is a hope that alters destiny. The kind of hope leaders are called upon to instill in others.

Martin Luther King, Jr. once said, "*If you lose hope, somehow you lose the vitality that keeps life moving, you lose that courage to be, that quality that helps you go on in spite of all. And so today I still have a dream.*"[19] Like Dr. King's said, we must recognize that hope is the water of life. You can suffer without it temporarily. But after a while, the lack of it brings death—maybe not physically, but at least in our minds and spirits. We must work to keep our hope reservoir full.

Scottish poet and novelist Robert Louis Stevenson (1850-1894) wrote the following poem to inspire hope within ourselves. It combines that which is transcendent and tangible into words explaining how we maintain reservoirs of hope:

Since Thou hast given me this good hope, O God,
That while my footsteps tread the flowery sod
And the great woods embower me, and white dawn
And purple even sweetly lead me on
From day to day and night to night, O God,
My life shall no wise miss the light of love,
But ever climbing, climb above
Man's one poor star, man's supine lands,
Into the azure steadfastness of death.
My life shall no wise lack the light of love,
My hands not lack the loving touch of hands,
But day by day, while yet I draw my breath,
And day by day unto my last of years,
I shall be one that has a perfect friend,
Her heart shall taste my laughter and my tears,
And her kind eyes shall lead me to the end.[20]

Principles for Reflection

• Hope is a specific and tangible expression of anticipating positive change for the future.

• The hope that we embrace is the hope that we will project to others. The opposite is also true.

• The most healthy organizations are built on hope—regardless of the environment or circumstances for which they operate.

• Hope is rational and should be evaluated and anticipated in a rational manner.

• There are always people among us who know more about hope than we can imagine. Read stories from Darfur, Rwanda, Afghanistan, or on the Holocaust for reminders about how we take hope for granted every day.

• Consider that hope is a gift we all have been given to be more than mere operators but instead instigators of life. As recipients of that gift, we must be honorable stewards of it as well.

UNIFICATION

"Man is his own most vexing problem."
— Reinhold Niebuhr

"I took a day to search for God, And found Him not; but as I trod, By rocky ledge, through woods untamed, Just where one scarlet lily flamed, I saw His footprint in the sod."
—William Bliss Carman

Seven instincts shape who we are as leaders. They encapsulate all of the social variety we exhibit to others, from the servant to the tyrant. Though they are integrated into our every thought and deed, we are relatively unaware of what they are or their impact on us. Perhaps the frenzied lives we lead are to blame, or maybe we spend too much time developing the veneer of leadership rather than excavating its core substance. No matter the cause, each day we are presented opportunities to make differences in the lives we touch. As we awaken to the reality that who we are on the inside has a direct role in what we project on the outside, we will have begun the process of apprehending untamed leadership.

We all drink from the same instinctual fountain—the same ad fontes of behavior. Yet, our commonality ends there. For though we are instinctively similar to each other, as well as some intelligent animals, we are actually part of a vast spectrum of diversity. This diversity exists because distinct thoughts, experiences, choices, memories, traditions, cultures, and people have shaped our dispositions over time. We think and act today because of a life-long instinctual sculpting process. Until now, this might have been hidden in the shadows of our psyches as our decisions and environment slowly chiseled out a form of conduct that we currently use. With our newfound awareness of these untamed instigators of behavior, everything changes. We can use what we now know and make efforts for positive change.

From the evidence at hand, our friends in the animal kingdom do not have this luxury. When they go against their untamed instincts, it often means survival is immediately in jeopardy. Still, as we have seen through numerous accounts and stories, animals are capable of extraordinary behavior transcending many of the assumptions we make of them. Some are able to stretch beyond the surly bonds of instinct and reshape their dispositions for behavior—all the while retaining what it means to be a dolphin, whale, ape, wolf, and so on. Their connection to instinct appears to be less muddled than ours, and their ability to collaborate, adapt, and negotiate within sustainable communities often seems more refined than our own. Although we often ignore the connections we share, there is much to be learned from animal instinct. They illuminate the very sources of why we behave the way we do.

American social writer and philosopher Eric Hoffer once said, "*To become different from what we are, we must have some awareness of what we are.*" Thus, as we reflect on what we are as individuals, communities, and organizations, we come to a new sense of possibility. We see the function and dysfunction of self-preservation, mimicry, communication, causality, rationality, duty, and hope. We find revelation in where we are and where we should be. We find what unites and disconnects us from each other.

However, awareness is not enough. We must take action, and this involves becoming fully engaged in the communities of people around us—gathering together to express needs, ideas, desires, and solutions. According to Proverbs 27:17, "*As iron sharpens iron, so a friend sharpens a friend.*"

As we reflect on what instincts have done and are doing to us, we must remember that progress cannot come from isolation. This might mean that we choose a group of diverse friends who are experts in their own fields and dedicate time to meeting with them routinely. It might mean we find one person who is our confidant and allow them to listen and critique our thoughts and actions. Whatever community we build and shape over our lives, it must be one that continually illumines the areas of our lives to which we are blinded.

During a tour of some caves near my home, a guide moves the group to an area void of any natural or man-made light. With his flashlight turned off, everyone stands in complete and utter darkness for several minutes. What happens is fascinating. With no light passing through their eyes, visitors can experience a condition called closed-eye hallucination. The cause is typically thermal noise-stimulating cells in the eye called photoreceptors. In the darkness, these excitations can actually be seen. In the absence of light, our bodies will create a faux image—even if it only appears as faded noise like on a television screen.

Similarly, isolated in our own darkness, we can be subject to hallucinations—images of leadership that are entirely fabricated. However, when we are engaged with community, we find tools and ideas that strengthen our ability to become aware of who we really are. Our reference points are no longer constructed within but instead have a place in a reality outside ourselves. A community of leaders looking at untamed leadership in this manner harnesses greater power. Like a wolf pack hunting, nurturing, protecting, and caring for itself, community is a unifying and self-correcting entity, and it has the ability to change the landscape of society.

Our untamed instincts are the sources of leadership. They are not a list of best practices. Nor are they a formula. They are merely the internal cogs and gears that shape our humanity. They will function without our awareness, and as such they might not lead us anywhere we would want to go. They will adapt to our environment but will not inform us of the changes that have been made. Untouched, they will allow us to simply be human and not much more. However, like a thoroughbred that was meant to run, when evaluated for their potential and trained to do great things, then we find a realm of leadership we never had previously discovered.

Untamed Leadership rests on one simple premise: we must never stop asking questions. Michael Marquardt contends in his book *Leading with Questions: How Leaders Find the Right Solutions by Knowing What to Ask*, "*Most leaders are unaware of the amazing power of questions, how they can generate short-term results and long-term learning and success. The problem is that we feel that we are supposed to have answers, not questions.*"[1] The benefit to a line of inquiry about what instigates our behavior is that we often learn more from the questions we ask than the answers we receive. We peel back assumptions made from years of reinforced behavior we never knew was there. We learn of people and situations that had greater effect on our lives than we expected. We find elements that quietly changed who we were simply by asking questions. With the examination of each strata that makes us who we are, we reckon with the past, see where we have changed or stayed stagnant, and then address what changes are necessary to move on. We become new leaders, new parents, and new forces within our community simply by examining instinct.

Humans are arguably one of the most cognitive and instinctual creatures on the planet. Yet, we are also often creatures of comfort and routine. This fact doesn't bode well for our pursuits of excellence in leadership. Aristotle once said, *"Excellence is an art won by training and habituation. We do not act rightly because we have virtue or excellence, but we rather have those because we have acted rightly. We are what we repeatedly do."*

Untamed leadership requires us to habitually step beyond what we are today in an awareness and a willingness for change. As we look at our animal neighbors, we can see how they are able to surpass established innate behavior to produce evidence of amazing dispositional change. If they are able to do so, what greater responsibility is it for us to be willing and able to do the same? This is where the ad fontes of leadership makes revolutionary transformation in our organizations. What we have learned about our behavior, we use. What we use becomes the water by which our followers are nourished and refreshed. As they draw upon the same fountain we have, they use what they learn, share it with others, and suddenly the efforts of one untamed leader creates cascading institutional, community, and societal change.

Several months after my first visit, I drove into the mountains to see my friends at the Wolf and Wildlife Center again. I sat for a long time watching an alpha male in his habitat interact with others in the pack.

None of them had to try to be great leaders. Nature was specifically conforming each of them to specific instincts and behavior. Some may ultimately be leaders of a couple, leaders of an entire pack, or not leaders at all. Like them, we all have the ability to harness our instincts. As we make efforts to understand our untamed instincts and shape their disposition, then we open up opportunities that were never available before. For us, it takes effort, practice, patience, and trial and error to understand how each instinct we have shapes who we are—but most of all it takes the willingness to think, change, and then act. Then, and only then, will we have connected with what it means to be untamed leaders.

The choice is ours, and with this new knowledge, the people we lead eagerly await our decision. 🐾

Notes

Prologue

[1]Mortimer, I. (2008). *The Time Traveler's Guide to Medieval England: A Handbook for Visitors to the Fourteenth Century*. New York: Bodley Head/Random House.

Introduction: Into the Wild

[1]For more information about the educational initiatives, research, and wolf habitants of the Wolf and Wildlife Center in Divide, CO, please see their website at: http://www.wolfeducation.org

[2]Wildlife Biologist and Wolf Reintroduction Expert Doug Smith. From NPR interview at *http://www.npr.org/templates/story/story.php?storyId=124501314*. More resources on his fascinating research are available at www.shoppbs.org

[3]James, W. (2007). *The Principles of Psychology*. New York: Cosimo Classics.

[4]Thorndike, E. (1913). *Educational Psychology (Vol. 1): The Original Nature of Man*. New York: Columbia University.

[5]McDougall, W. (1915). *An Introduction to Social Psychology*. Ontario: Batoche Books.

[6]Maslow, A. (1943). A Theory of Human Motivation. *Psychological Review, 50(4)*, 370–96.

[7]Kringelbach M.L., Lehtonen A., Squire S., Harvey A.G., Craske M.G., et al. (2008). A Specific and Rapid Neural Signature for Parental Instinct. *PLoS ONE 3(2)*.

Instinct #1: Self-Preservation

[1]See the following link for the National Geographic footage of a bull elephant defending a newborn from an entire tribe of lions: *http://www.youtube.com/watch?v=7v2hZAq0lbQ*. Additionally, see how female elephants work together to save a drowning infant: *http://www.youtube.com/watch?v=Cd-LtWtNvDw*

[2]Curwin, L. (2010). Train kills elephants trying to protect young in India. Retrieved October 7, 2010, from *http://www.digitaljournal.com/article/298042*

[3]CNN.com. (1996). Gorilla Rescues Child. Retrieved December 9, 2010, from *http://www.cnn.com/EVENTS/1996/year.in.review/talk/gorilla/gorilla.html*

[4]Norris, K. (1978). *Whales, Dolphins, and Porpoises.* Berkeley: University of California Press.

[5]Blair, T. (2010). *A Journey: My Political Life.* New York: Knopf.

[6]Military Times (2010). Awards and Citations: James H. Fields, Medal of Honor. Retrieved from *http://militarytimes.com/citations-medals-awards/recipient.php?recipientid=1568*

[7]Aspen Institute. (2010). Mission Statement. Retrieved November 15, 2010, from *www.aspeninstitute.org.*

[8]Yaverbaum, E. (2004). *Leadership Secrets of the World's Most Successful CEOs.* Chicago: Dearborn Trade Pub.

[9]Fleming, P. and Zyglidopoulos, S.C. (2009). *Charting Corporate Corruption : Agency, Structure, and Escalation.* Northampton, MA: Edward Elgar.

Instinct #2: Mimicry

[1]Fairhurst, G. T. (2010). *The Power of Framing.* San Francisco: Jossey-Bass.

[2]Marler, P. (1957). Specific Distinctiveness in the Communication Signals of Birds. *Behavior, 6–11(1),* 13–39.

[3]Lorenz, K. (1981). *The Foundations of Ethology.* New York: Simon & Schuster.

[4]Linden, E. (2002). *The Octopus and the Orangutan: More True Tales of Animal Intrigue, Intelligence, and Ingenuity.* New York: Penguin.

[5]Doughty, R. (1988). *The Mockingbird.* Austin: University of Texas Press.

[6]Langridge, K.V., Broom, M., Osorio, D. (2007). Selective Signaling by Cuttlefish to Predators. *Current Biology, 17(24),* R1044–R1045.

[7]Zeller, A. (2002). Pretending in Monkeys. In R.W. Mitchell (Ed.). *Pretending and Imagination in Animals and Children,* 183–195. Cambridge, MA: Cambridge University Press.

[8]Williams, K. D., J. P. Forgas, et al. (2005). *The Social Outcast: Ostracism, Social Exclusion, Rejection, and Bullying.* New York: Psychology Press.

[9]The Stolen Valor Act of 2005 can be downloaded from the Library of Congress from: *http://thomas.loc.gov/cgi-bin/bdquery/z?d109:SN01998:@@@D&summ2=m&*

[10]King, I. (2008). Broadcom Executive Wasn't Awarded His Degrees, University Says. Retrieved October 14, 2010, from *http://www.bloomberg.com/apps/news?pid=newsarchive&sid=aX6ktZQsKoQ4&refer=home*

[11]Bailenson, J.N., Yee, N., Patel, K., & Beall, A.C. (2007). Detecting Digital Chameleons. Computers in Human *Behavior, 24,* 66–87.

[12]Clarke, T. (2004). *Ask Not: The Inauguration of John F. Kennedy and the Speech that Changed America.* New York: Henry Holt and Co.

[13]Sommer, S. (2005). *John F. Kennedy: His Life and Legacy.* New York: Harper Collins.

Instinct #3: Communication

[1]Maxwell, J. C. (2010). *Everyone Communicates, Few Connect: What the Most Effective People Do Differently.* Nashville, TN: Thomas Nelson.

[2]From interview on June 16, 2010. Visit *http://www.cmzoo.com* for more details about the wonderful animal behavior research that is being done at this zoo.

[3]Morton, A. (2002). *Listening to Whales: What the Orcas Have Taught Us.* New York: Ballantine Pubishing.

[4]Rue, L. L. (1997). *The Deer of North America.* New York: Lyons & Burford, Publishers.

[5]Vaughan, T. A., J. M. Ryan, et al. (2000). *Mammalogy.* Fort Worth: Saunders College Pub.

[6]Sanborn, M. (2006). *You Don't Need a Title to Be a Leader: How Anyone, Anywhere, Can Make a Positive Difference.* New York: Crown Business.

[7]Nicholson, N. (2000). *Executive Instinct: Managing the Human Animal in the Information Age.* New York: Crown Business.

[8]Bowlby, J. (1992). *Attachment and Loss.* New York: Basic Books.

[9]Hall, E. (1959). *The Silent Language.* New York: Doubleday.

[10]Waters, T. (2006). *Class 11: Inside the CIA's First Post-9/11 Spy Class.* New York: Dutton.

[11]Mehrabian, A., & Ferris, S. (1967). Inference of Attitudes from Nonverbal Communication in Two Channels. *Journal of Consulting Psychology, 31(3)*, 248–258.

[12]Kolditz, T. (2007). *In Extremis Leadership: Leading as if Your Life Depended on It.* San Francisco: Jossey-Bass.

[13]Charteris-Black, J. (2006). *The Communication of Leadership: The Design of Leadership Style.* London, New York: Routledge.

[14]Zito, K. (2001). Game Rivals Ready for Console Combat. Retrieved October 12, 2010, from *http://articles.sfgate.com/2001-05-18/business/17599188_1_sony-computer-entertainment-microsoft-nintendo-and-sony-consoles*

Instinct #4: Causality

[1]Huck, S. (1979). *Rival Hypotheses: Alternative Interpretations of Data Based Conclusions.* New York: Harper Collins College Publishing.

[2]Spotts, P. (2010). Universe might hold three times more stars than previously thought. Retrieved December 17, 2010, from *http://www.csmonitor.com/Science/2010/1201/Universe-might-hold-three-times-more-stars-than-previously-thought*

[3]Dickinson, A. (1980). *Contemporary Animal Learning Theory.* New York: Cambridge University Press.

[4]Shanks, N. (2002). *Animals and Science: A Guide to the Debates.* Santa Barbara, CA: ABC-CLIO.

[5]Shettleworth, S. J. (2010). *Cognition, Evolution, and Behavior.* New York: Oxford University Press.

[6]Castro, L. and Wasserman, E. A. (2010). Animal Learning. *Wiley Interdisciplinary Reviews: Cognitive Science, 1,* 89–98.

[7]Taylor, A. H., G. R. Hunt, et al. (2009). Do New Caledonian crows solve physical problems through causal reasoning? *Proc Biol Sci, 276(1655),* 247–254.

[8]Mech, L. D. and L. Boitani (2003). *Wolves: Behavior, Ecology, and Conservation.* Chicago: University of Chicago Press.

[9]2007 America's Cup Race. Available at *http://www.intersail.co.uk/news/?article=137124*

[10]Fleming, T. (1999). Unlikely Victory: Thirteen Ways the Americans Could Have Lost the Revolution. In Robert Crowley, *What If: The Worlds Foremost Military Historians Imagine What Might Have Been.* New York: Berkeley Books, 171–172.

[11]National Maritime Museum (1976). *1776 The British Story of the American Revolution.* London: National Maritime Museum.

[12]Hance, J. (2009). *Chaos, Confusion, and Political Ignorance: June 28 – August 5, 1914: The Untold truth About the Start of World War II.* Pittsburgh: Dorrance Publishing Company.

[13]Beyer, R. and History Channel (2008). *The Greatest Stories Never Told: 230 Tales From History to Astonish, Bewilder, and Stupefy.* Pleasantville: Readers Digest Association.

[14]Griffiths, W.R. (2003). *The Great War.* Garden City Park: Square One Publishers.

[15]Lansing, A. (1959). *Endurance: Shackleton's Incredible Voyage.* New York: Basic Books.

[16]Shackleton, E. H. (2001). *South: The Story of Shackleton's Last Expedition, 1914–1917.* Edinburgh: Birlinn.

[17]Caswell, C. (2004). *The Greatest Sailing Stories Ever Told*. Guilford, CT: Lyon's Press.

[18]Morris, B. (2008). Steve Jobs Speaks Out. Retrieved October 9, 2010, from *http://money.cnn.com/galleries/2008/fortune/0803/gallery.jobsqna.fortune/6.html*

Instinct #5: Rationality

[1]Kenneally, C. (2007). *The First Word: The Search for the Origins of Language*. New York: Viking.

[2]Herman, L. (2006). *Intelligence and Rational Behaviour in the Bottle-nosed Dolphin. Rational Animals*. ed. Susan Hurley. New York: Oxford University Press.

[3]Premack, D., & G. Woodruff. (1978). Does the chimpanzee have a theory of mind? *The Behavioral and Brain Sciences, 4*, 515–526.

[4]Miri, S. (2004). *Rationality and Tribal Thought*. New Delhi: Mittal Publications.

[5]Gilovich, T. (1991). *How We Know What Isn't So: The Fallibility of Human Reason in Everyday Life*. New York: Free Press.

[6]Dotlich, D. L. and P. C. Cairo (2003). *Why CEOs Fail: The 11 Behaviors that can Derail Your Climb to the Top—And How to Manage Them*. San Francisco: Jossey-Bass.

[7]Irwin, T. (2009). *Derailed: Five Lessons Learned from Catastrophic Failures of Leadership*. Nashville: Thomas Nelson.

[8]Bennis, W. G. (2003). *On Becoming a Leader*. Cambridge, MA: Perseus Pub.

[9]Waters, J. (2007). Nardelli's arrogance led to downfall at Home Depot. Retrieved July 13, 2010, from *http://www.marketwatch.com/story/nardellis-arrogance-led-to-downfall-analysts*

[10]Shelton, Charlotte K. and Darling, J. R. (2001). The quantum skills model in management: a new paradigm to enhance effective leadership. *Leadership and Organization Development Journal, 22 (6)*, 264–273.

[11]Dickmann, M. H. and Stanford-Blair, N. (2002). *Connecting Leadership to the Brain*. Thousand Oaks, CA: Corwin Press.

[12]From Interview on January 22, 2010. For more information on the great work being done by the North Dakota Indian Affairs Commission, visit: *http://www.nd.gov/indianaffairs*

[13]Bennis, W. G. and Nanus, B. (1997). *Leaders: Strategies for Taking Charge*. New York: HarperBusiness.

[14]Stack, J. (1992). *The Great Game of Business*. New York: Doubleday.

[15]Force, J. (2009). Questioning: The Art of Asking Dumb Questions. Retrieved October 10, 2010, from *http://www.banffcentre.ca/departments/.../library/.../creative_questioning.pdf*

Instinct #6: Duty

[1]Valéry, P. and Gifford, P. (2000). *Cahiers / Notebooks.* Frankfurt am Main. New York: P. Lang.

[2]Kant, I. (2004). *Critique of Practical Reason.* Mineola, NY: Dover Publications.

[3]Cottingham, J. (1996). *Western Philosophy: An Anthology.* Oxford, OX, UK; Cambridge, MA, USA: Blackwell Publishers.

[4]See the Dolphin Rescue at Hawkes Bay *http://www. youtube.com/watch?v=75MC2HEmpy4 dolphin*

[5]Howard, C. J. (1995). *Dolphin Chronicles: A Fascinating, Moving Tale of One Woman's Quest to Understand—And Communicate With—The Sea's Most Mysterious Creatures.* New York: Bantam Books.

[6]Merriam-Webster Inc. (2010). *Merriam-Webster's Dictionary for Children.* Springfield, MA: Merriam-Webster.

[7]Interview of Todd Endris. Downloaded December 12, 2010, from *http://www.surfingmagazine.com/ news/great-white-shark-attack-monterrey-todd-endris-090207/*

[8]Interview of Todd Endris. Available for viewing at *http://today.msnbc.msn.com/id/21689083/ns/today-today_people/*

[9]Thomson, A. (2010). Dolphins saved us from shark, lifeguards say. Downloaded December 12, 2010, from *http://www.nzherald.co.nz/nz/news/article.cfm?c_ id=1&objectid=3613343*

[10]Anda, R. (2008). Dolphins save Palawan fisherman. Downloaded December 12, 2010, from *http://newsinfo. inquirer.net/inquirerheadlines/nation/view/20081217-178401/Dolphins-save-Palawan-fisherman*

[11]Dick Van Dyke Saved by Porpoises. Downloaded December 11, 2010, from *http://www.telegraph.co.uk/ news/worldnews/northamerica/usa/8124734/Dick-Van-Dyke-saved-by-porpoises.html*

[12]Bellamy, R. and Ross, A. (1996). *A Textual Introduction to Social and Political Theory*. Manchester, New York: Manchester University Press.

[13]Sullenberger, C. and J. Zaslow (2009). *Highest Duty: My Search for What Really Matters*. New York: William Morrow.

[14]United States Army (2010). Army Leadership: Competent, Confident, and Agile. Retrieved April 14, 2010, from *http://www.fas.org/irp/doddir/army/fm6-22.pdf*

[15]Walzer, M. (1977). *Just and Unjust Wars: A Moral Argument with Historical Illustrations*. New York: Basic Books.

[16]Sweetman, J. (2001). *Essential Histories: The Crimean War*. London: Osprey Publishing.

[17]Sears, S. (2004). *Gettysburg*. New York: First Mariner Books.

[18]United States Army (2010). Non-Commissioned Officer Creed. Retrieved April 14, 2010 from *http:// usacac.army.mil/cac2/cal/creeds.html#nco*

[19]United States Army (2010). Soldier's Creed. Retrieved April 14, 2010 from *http://usacac.army.mil/cac2/cal/creeds.html#s*

[20]Christian Leadership Academy. (2010). List of Principles of the Christian Faith. Retrieved July 23, 2010 from *http://www.christianleadershipacademy.org/HonorCode*

[21]Lowen, A. (1985). *Narcissism: Denial of the True Self.* New York: Collier Books.

[22]Maccoby, M. (2000). Narcissistic Leaders: The Incredible Pros, the Inevitable Consequences. Downloaded December 1, 2010, from *http://www.maccoby.com/Articles/NarLeaders.shtml*

[23]Amnesty International. (2010). Starving North Koreans forced to survive on diet of grass and bark. Downloaded December 5, 2010, from *http://www.amnesty-usa.org/document.php?id=ENGNAU20100715176876 lang=e*

[24]North Korean Economic Watch, satellite images, available at *http://www.nkeconwatch.com/north-korea-uncovered-google-earth/*

[25]Yukl, G. A. (2010). *Leadership in Organizations.* Upper Saddle River, NJ: Prentice Hall.

[26]Collins, J. C. (2001). *Good to Great: Why Some Companies Make the Leap—And Others Don't.* New York: Harper Business.

[27]Wheatley, M. (2002). *Turning to One Another: Simple Conversations to Restore Hope to the Future.* New York: Berrett-Koehler Publishers.

[28]Blanchard, K., & Hodges, P. (2005). *Lead Like Jesus: Lessons for Everyone From the Greatest Leadership Role Model of All Time.* Nashville: Thomas Nelson.

[29]Irving, W. (1994). *George Washington: A Biography.* New York: Da Capo Press.

Instinct #7: Hope

[1]Carr, A. (2004). *Positive Psychology: The Science of Happiness and Human Strengths.* Hove, New York: Brunner-Routledge.

[2]Knowles, R. T. and G. F. McLean (1992). *Psychological foundations of moral education and character development: an integrated theory of moral development.* Washington DC Council for Research in Values and Philosophy.

[3]Fluker, W. E. (2008). *Ethical Leadership: The Quest for Character, Civility, and Community.* Minneapolis, MN: Fortress Press.

[4]Bavidge, M. and I. Ground (1994). *Can We Understand Animal Minds?* New York: St. Martin's Press.

[5]Masson, J. M. and S. McCarthy (1995). *When Elephants Weep: The Emotional Lives of Animals.* New York: Delacorte Press.

[6]Mitchell, R. W. and Thompson, N.S. (1997). *Anthropomorphism, Anecdotes, and Animals.* Albany: State University of New York Press, 385.

[7]Kelsey, E. (2009). *Watching Giants: The Secret Lives of Whales.* Berkeley: University of California Press.

[8]Midgley, M. (1984). *Animals and Why They Matter.* Athens: University of Georgia Press.

[9]Snyder, C., Rand, K., & Sigmon, D. (2002). Hope Theory, A Member of the Positive Psychology Family. In C. Snyder & S. Lopez (Eds.), *Handbook of Positive Psychology.* (257–276). New York: Oxford University Press.

[10]Bateman, T., & Porath, C. (2003). Transcendent Behavior. In K. Cameron, J. Dutton, & R. Quinn (Eds.), *Positive Organizational Scholarship: Foundations of a New Discipline.* San Francisco: Berrett-Koehler Publishers.

[11]Kaplan, M. A. (1998). *Between Dignity and Despair: Jewish Life in Nazi Germany.* New York: Oxford University Press.

[12]Zullo, A. and M. Bovsun (2004). *Survivors: True Stories of Children in the Holocaust.* New York: Scholastic.

[13]Gallup Management Journal. (2003). Gallup Study Indicates Actively Disengaged Workers Cost U.S. Hundreds of Billions Each Year. Retrieved December 17, 2010, from *http://gmj.gallup.com/content/466/gallup-study-indicates-actively-disengaged-workers-cost-us-hundreds.aspx*

[14]Reagan, R. (1984). Remarks at a Reagan-Bush Rally in St. Louis, Missouri. Retrieved February 22, 2010, from *http://www.reagan.utexas.edu/archives/speeches/1984/110484b.htm*

[15]Edwards, L. (2005). *The Essential Ronald Reagan: A Profile in Courage, Justice, and Wisdom.* Lanham: Rowman & Littlefield.

[16]Hodge, C., & Nolan, C. (2007). *U.S. Presidents and Foreign Policy.* Santa Barbara: ABC-CLIO.

[17]Wheatley, M. (2002). *Turning to One Another: Simple Conversations to Restore Hope to the Future.* New York: Berrett-Koehler Publishers.

[18]Mbegu Trust (2010). The Leadership We Need to Build the Kenya and Africa We Want: Mbegu Trust 'Lead On' Competition Articles. Retrieved September 2, 2010 from *http://www.mbegutrust.org/images/YKL-winners.pdf*

[19]Washington, J. (1990). *A Testament of Hope: The Essential Writings and Speeches of Martin Luther King, Jr.* New York: HarperOne.

[20]Stephenson, R. (2009). *Poems Volume II: Cambridge Scholars Publishing Classic Texts.* Newcastle: Cambridge Scholars Publishing.

Conclusion: Unification

[1]Marquardt, M. (2005). *Leading with Questions: How Leaders Find the Right Solutions By Knowing What To Ask.* San Francisco: Jossey-Bass.

RESOURCES

Animal Behavior and Instincts

Allison, P. (2008). *Whatever You Do, Don't Run: True Tales of a Botswana Safari Guide.* Guilford, CT: Lyons Press.

Bekoff, M., & Pierce, J. (2009). *Wild Justice: The Moral Lives of Animals.* Chicago: The University of Chicago Press.

Bingley, T. (1840). *Stories Illustrative of the Instincts of Animals.* London: Charles Fleet.

Childs, C. (2007). *The Animal Dialogues: Uncommon Encounters in the Wild.* New York: Little, Brown.

Corbett, J. (1990). *Jungle Lore.* Delhi: Oxford University Press.

Dugatkin, L. A. (2009). *Principles of Animal Behavior.* New York: W. W. Norton.

French, T. (2010). *Zoo Story: Life in the Garden of Captives.* New York: Hyperion.

Heinsohn, R., & Packer, C. (1995). Complex cooperative strategies in group-territorial African lions. *Science, 269(5228),* 1260–1262.

Linden, E. (2002). *The Octopus and the Orangutan: More True Tales of Animal Intrigue, Intelligence, and Ingenuity.* New York: Dutton.

Lloyd, J., & Mitchinson, J. (2007). *The Book of Animal Ignorance.* New York: Harmony Books.

Lorenz, K. (1981). *The Foundations of Ethology.* New York: Springer-Verlag New York.

Mackintosh, N. J. (1994). *Animal Learning and Cognition.* San Diego: Academic Press.

Markle, S. (2009). *Animal Heroes: True Rescue Stories.* Minneapolis, MN: Millbrook Press.

Morton, A. (2002). *Listening to Whales: What the Orcas Have Taught Us.* New York: Ballantine.

Robinson, P. T. (2004). *Life at the Zoo: Behind the Scenes with the Animal Doctors.* New York: Columbia University Press.

Zullo, A. (2001). *True Tales of Animal Heroes.* Mahwah: Troll.

Human Behavior Development

Berk, L.E. (2001). *Awakening Children's Minds.* Oxford University Press.

Goncu, A. and Gaskins, S. (Eds.) (2007). *Play and Development: Evolutionary, Sociocultural and Functional Perspectives.* Mahwah, NJ: Erlbaum Press.

Gosso, Y., De Lima Salum E Morais, M. & Otta, E. (2007). Pretend play of Brazilian children: a window into different cultural worlds. *Journal of Cross-Cultural Psychology, 38(5)*, 53.

Hauser, M. D. and Wolfe, N. (1994). Language Comprehension in Ape and Child Monograph No. 233. *American Anthropologist, 96(3)*, 745–747.

Lillard, A., Nishida, T., Massaro, D. & Vaish, A. (2007). Further examination of the behavioral signs of pretense. *Infancy 11(1)*, 1.

Meyers, G. (2007). *The Significance of Children and Animals.* Indiana: Purdue University Press.

Reese, E., Hayne, H., & MacDonald, S. (2008). Looking Back to the Future: Mäori and Pakeha Mother-Child Birth Stories. *Child Development, 79(1)*, 114–125.

Singer, D., Golinkoff, R. M., & Hirsh-Pasek, K. (Eds.) (2006). *Play=Learning: How Play Motivates and Enhances Children's Cognitive and Social-emotional Growth.* New York: Oxford University Press.

Sun, Y., Pan, Z., & Shen, L. (2008). Understanding the third-person perception: Evidence from a meta-analysis. *Journal of Communication, 58*, 280–300.

Cognitive and Behavior

Axelrod, R. (2008). *The Complexity of Cooperation: Agent-based Models of Competition and Collaboration.* Princeton, NJ: Princeton University Press.

Bateson, G. (2000). *Steps to an Ecology of Mind.* Chicago: University of Chicago Press.

Browne, M. N., & Keeley, S. M. (2001). *Asking the Right Questions: A Guide to Critical Thinking.* Upper Saddle River, NJ: Prentice Hall.

Force, J. (2000). Creative Questioning: The art of asking dumb questions. Retrieved October 11, 2010, from *http://www.banffcentre.ca/departments/leadership/library/pdf/creative_questioning.pdf*

Francis, R. C. (2004). *Why Men Won't Ask for Directions: The Seductions of Sociobiology.* Princeton, NJ: Princeton University Press.

Gagné, L. (2007). Non-rational compliance with social norms: sincere and hypocritical. *Social Science Information, 46(3),* 445.

Goldstein, N. J., Martin, S. J., & Cialdini, R. B. (2010). *Yes! 50 Scientifically Proven Ways to be Persuasive.* New York: Free Press.

Gonzales, L. (2003). *Deep Survival: Who Lives, Who Dies, and Why; True Stories of Miraculous Endurance and Sudden Death.* New York: W.W. Norton.

Huck, S. W., & Sandler, H. M. (1979). *Rival hypotheses: alternative interpretations of data based conclusions.* New York: Harper & Row.

Kunda, Z. (1999). *Social Cognition: Making Sense of People.* Cambridge, MA: MIT Press.

Lansing, A. (1959). *Endurance: Shackleton's Incredible Voyage.* New York: McGraw-Hill.

Layder, D. (2004). *Social and Personal Identity: Understanding Yourself.* London: Sage Publications.

Lehrer, J. (2009). *How We Decide.* Boston: Houghton Mifflin Harcourt.

Mawson, A. R. (2005). Understanding Mass Panic and Other Collective Responses to Threat and Disaster. *Psychiatry: Interpersonal Biological Processes, 68(2),* 95–113.

McDougall, W. (1960). *An Introduction to Social Psychology.* London: Methuen.

Mehrabian, A., & Ferris, S. R. (1967). Inference Of Attitudes From Nonverbal Communication In Two Channels. *Journal of Consulting Psychology, 31(3),* 248–252.

Myers, D. G. (1993). *Social Psychology.* New York: McGraw-Hill.

Newberg, A. B., & Waldman, M. R. (2006). *Why We Believe What We Believe.* New York: Free Press.

Perrow, C. (1999). *Normal Accidents: Living with High-risk Technologies.* Princeton, NJ: Princeton University Press.

Pink, D. H. (2009). *Drive: The Surprising Truth About What Motivates Us.* New York: Riverhead Books.

Tannen, D. (1994). *Talking From 9 to 5.* New York: W. Morrow.

Tinbergen, N. (1969). *The Study of Instinct.* Oxford: Clarendon P.

Veblen, T. (2004). *The Instinct of Workmanship*. London: Routledge/Thoemmes.

Vedantam, S. (2010). *The Hidden Brain: How Our Unconscious Minds Elect Presidents, Control Markets, Wage Wars, and Save Our Lives*. New York: Spiegel & Grau.

Weiss, A.P. (1920). Psychology, From the Standpoint of the Behaviorist. *Psychological Bulletin, 17(8)*, 266–270.

Organizational Behavior and Adaptation

Barker, J. A. (1989). *Discovering the Future: The Business of Paradigms*. St. Paul, MN: ILI Press.

Battram, A. (1998). *Navigating Complexity*. London: The Industrial Society.

Bennet, A., & Bennet, D. (2004). *Organizational Survival in the New World: The Intelligent Complex Adaptive System*. Amsterdam: Butterworth-Heinemann.

Bosch, L. (2004, Winter). Self-Sustaining Organizations and Leadership. Retrieved September 14, 2010, *www.banffcentre.ca/departments/leadership/library/pdf/self-sustaining_organizations_and_leadership.pdf*

Dolan, S., Garcia, S., & Auerbach, A. (2003). Understanding and managing chaos in organisations. *International Journal of Management, 20(1)*, 23-35.

Dixit, A. K., & Nalebuff, B. (2008). *The Art of Strategy: A Game Theorist's Guide to Success in Business & Life*. New York: W.W. Norton.

Elliott, E. W., & Kiel, L. D. (2001). *Chaos Theory in the Social Sciences: Foundations and Applications*. Ann Arbor: University of Michigan Press.

Fisher, L. (2008). *Rock, Paper, Scissors: Game Theory in Everyday Life*. New York: Basic Books.

Gallwey, W. T. (2000). *The Inner Game of Work*. New York: Random House.

Hatch, M. J., & Cunliffe, A. L. (2006). *Organization Theory: Modern, Symbolic, and Postmodern Perspectives*. New York: Oxford University Press.

Kellerman, B. (1999). *Reinventing Leadership: Making the Connection Between Politics and Business*. Albany, NY: State University of New York Press.

Kreitner, R., Kinicki, A., & Cole, N. (2003). *Fundamentals of Organizational Behaviour: Key Concepts, Skills & Best Practices*. Toronto: McGraw-Hill Ryerson.

Mazany, P. (1995). *Team Think: Team New Zealand: The "Black Magic" of Management Behind the 1995 America's Cup Success*. Auckland, NZ: VisionPlus Developments.

Olson, E. E., & Eoyang, G. H. (2001). *Facilitating Organization Change: Lessons from Complexity Science*. San Francisco, CA: Jossey-Bass/Pfeiffer.

Solansky, S. T. (2008). Leadership Style and Team Processes in Self-Managed Teams. *Journal of Leadership & Organizational Studies, 14(4)*, 332–341.

Stacey, R. D. (1992). *Managing the Unknowable: Strategic Boundaries Between Order and Chaos in Organizations*. San Francisco: Jossey-Bass.

Stacey, R. D., Griffin, D., & Shaw, P. (2000). *Complexity and Management: Fad or Radical Challenge to Systems Thinking?* London: Routledge.

Wheatley, M. J. (2006). *Leadership and the New Science: Discovering Order in a Chaotic World*. San Francisco, CA: Berrett-Koehler.

Non-traditional Leadership

Boyatzis, R. E., & McKee, A. (2005). *Resonant Leadership: Renewing Yourself and Connecting with Others through Mindfulness, Hope, and Compassion*. Boston: Harvard Business School Press.

Goleman, D., Boyatzis, R. E., & MacKee, A. (2006). *Primal Leadership*. Boston, MA: Harvard Business School Press.

Hetland, H., Sandal, G. M., & Johnsen, T. B. (2008). Followers' Personality and Leadership. *Journal of Leadership & Organizational Studies, 14(4)*, 322–331.

Howell, J. P., & Costley, D. L. (2006). *Understanding Behaviors for Effective Leadership*. Upper Saddle River, NJ: Pearson Prentice Hall.

Kellerman, B. (2004). *Bad Leadership: What it is, How it Happens, Why it Matters*. Boston: Harvard Business.

Kellerman, B. (2010). *Leadership: Essential Selections*

on Power, Authority, and Influence. New York: Mc-Graw-Hill.

Kolditz, T. A. (2007). *In Extremis Leadership: Leading as if Your Life Depended on It.* San Francisco: Jossey-Bass.

Kotter, J. P. (2008). *A Sense of Urgency.* Boston: Harvard Business.

Levy, D. A., Parco, J. E. and Blass, F. R. (2009). *The 52nd Floor: Thinking Deeply about Leadership.* Montgomery: Enso Books.

MacLeod, H. (2009). *Ignore Everybody: And 39 Other Keys to Creativity.* New York: Portfolio.

Maxwell, J. C. (2005). *The 360° Leader: Developing Your Influence From Anywhere in the Organization.* Nashville: Nelson Business.

Nicholson, N. (2000). *Executive Instinct: Managing the Human Animal in the Information Age.* New York: Crown Business.

Prochaska, F. (2007). *Metamind: Think and Lead; The Connection Between Being and Doing.* Ann Arbor: Copley Custom Textbooks.

Sanborn, M. (2006). *You Don't Need a Title to be a Leader: How Anyone, Anywhere, Can Make a Positive Difference.* New York: Currency Doubleday.

Yaverbaum, E. (2004). *Leadership Secrets of the World's Most Successful CEOs.* Chicago: Dearborn Trade Pub.

Yukl, G. A. (1981). *Leadership in Organizations*. Englewood Cliffs, NJ: Prentice-Hall.

Leadership within the Context of History

Ambrose, S. E. (1996). *Undaunted Courage: Meriwether Lewis, Thomas Jefferson, and the Opening of the American West*. New York: Simon & Schuster.

Barefoot, C. (2002). *Thomas Jefferson on Leadership: Executive Lessons from his Life and Letters*. New York: Plume.

Bradley, J., & Cowley, R. (2002). *More What If?: Eminent Historians Imagine What Might Have Been*. London: Macmillan.

Bradley, J., & Cowley, R. (2001). *What If? 2: Eminent Historians Imagine What Might Have Been Essays*. New York: Putnam.

Cowley, R., & Ambrose, S. E. (1999). *What If?* New York: Putnam.

Davis, B. (1996). *The Civil War: Strange and Fascinating Facts*. New York: Wings Books.

Fawcett, B. (2006). *How to Lose a Battle: Foolish Plans and Great Military Blunders*. New York: Harper.

Jenkinson, C. (2004). *Becoming Jefferson's People: Reinventing the American Republic in the Twenty-first Century*. Reno: Marmarth Press.

Jones, L. B. (1995). *Jesus, CEO: Using Ancient Wisdom for Visionary Leadership*. New York: Hyperion.

Karnow, S. (1984). *Vietnam: A History.* New York: Penguin Books.

Lewis, M., Clark, W., & De, V. B. (1997). *The Journals of Lewis and Clark.* Boston: Houghton Mifflin.

Mortimer, I. (2010). *The Time Traveler's Guide to Medieval England: A Handbook for Visitors to the Fourteenth Century.* New York: Simon & Schuster.

Naylor, S. (2005). *Not a Good Day to Die: The Untold Story of Operation Anaconda.* New York: Berkley Books.

Phillips, D. T. (1993). *Lincoln on Leadership: Executive Strategies for Tough Times.* New York: Warner Books.

Trethewey, A., & Goodall, H. (2007). Leadership Reconsidered as Historical Subject: Sketches from the Cold War to Post-9/11. *Leadership, 3(4),* 457–477.

Zullo, A. and Bovsun, M. (2004). *Survivors: True Stories of Children in the Holocaust.* New York: Scholastic.

Acknowledgments

The scope of this book clearly put me in a realm of untested waters. Coalescing ideas from often polarized fields into a working synergy was only possible by talking to professionals in many areas of research and practice. As a result, I reached out to some of the most experienced and scholarly individuals in their fields to help me see the concepts of instinctual leadership through their own eyes. This list of appreciation barely touches on all of the contributors to this effort, but I would like to recognize the following individuals for their specific support.

In the realm of animal behavior, I would like to express my thanks to Darlene Kobobel of the Wolf and Wildlife Center in Colorado for continual access to the center's wolves, as well as her insight into wolf behavior and intelligence.

In a very short time, I was fortunate to build a partnership with Debbie Heineman of the Wolf Conservation Center in South Salem, NY. Thank you, Debbie, for your support, encouragement, and assistance in promoting this book.

Animal behaviorist Megan Sanders of the Cheyenne Mountain Zoo provided many useful stories and expertise in the challenges of animal behavior research. Thank you for your time, Megan.

In the realm of leadership, I could not have initiated and found early momentum in this project without the help of award-winning author and scholar of the *Thomas Jefferson Hour*, Clay Jenkinson. Thank you for offering so many hours of stunning insight into the leadership paradigms at the birth of our nation.

I would like to thank Executive Director of the North Dakota Indian Affairs Commission, Scott Davis, who provided a wealth of detail about the challenges of leadership in indigenous and Native American societies.

T.J. Waters, author of *Class 11: My Story Inside the CIA's First Post-9/11 Spy Class*, was a key asset in my research of military and government agencies. Thank you, Tom, for spending hours with me on the phone.

Steven Carter was a critical resource for understanding the challenges of leadership within the lower ranks and higher echelon of the U.S. military. Thank you, Steve, for your important contributions to this project and your immense understanding of human behavior and military history. Some individuals are unable to be recognized by name due to their current military or government operational status, but I would be amiss if I didn't reference their significant contributions to this project.

My editors Jim Parco, Dave Levy, and all those at Enso Books made this project possible. You have my sincere gratitude for holding me to a quality effort while still being amiable, enlightening, and patient. Your wisdom in this process is only superseded by your professionalism.

On a personal note, the thousands of hours of research, writing, library weekends, and conference calls could not have been possible without my wife's and parents' support. Thank you for giving me the ability to keep this project on the priority list. The effort is as equally yours as it is mine. Also, thank you to my extended family and in-laws for your consistent encouragement.

Advance Praise for
Untamed Leadership

The wolves of the Wolf Conservation Center teach us lessons every day about what it means to be an effective and fair leader, to control the pack with just a glance or a subtle gesture. Hopefully the greater human population will glean a similar and valuable lesson from Dr. Carter's insightful book.

Debbie Heineman
Executive Director, Wolf Conservation Center

My professional role is such that honing my leadership capabilities, and finding new angles on leadership, is truly important. **Untamed Leadership** *offers a thought-provoking perspective and several terrific new avenues to pursue.*

Joe Sprague
Vice President of Marketing, Alaska Airlines

As it has always been, nature holds the keys to our interactions with others and the role we choose to play. **Untamed Leadership** *is very insightful and provocative reading.*

Darlene Kobobel
Founder, Colorado Wolf and Wildlife Center

Dr. Carter takes a thought provoking look at parallels between animal and human behavior. Through insightful and often entertaining anecdotes he offers insight and a point of view on ourselves that many may not have previously considered.

Megan Sanders
Animal Behavior Programs Manager
Cheyenne Mountain Zoo

CPSIA information can be obtained at www.ICGtesting.com
Printed in the USA
BVOW021246181211

278629BV00002B/2/P